Maxwell Yesof

Chennai,

India

27. 3. 08

Mahabalipuram

Monumental Legacy

Series Editor: Devangana Desai

Monumental Legacy

MAHABALIPURAM
(Mamallapuram)

R. Nagaswamy

OXFORD
UNIVERSITY PRESS

OXFORD
UNIVERSITY PRESS

YMCA Library Building, Jai Singh Road, New Delhi 110 001

Oxford University Press is a department of the University of Oxford.
It furthers the University's objective of excellence in research, scholarship,
and education by publishing worldwide in

Oxford New York
Auckland Cape Town Dar es Salaam Hong Kong Karachi
Kuala Lumpur Madrid Melbourne Mexico City Nairobi
New Delhi Shanghai Taipei Toronto

With offices in
Argentina Austria Brazil Chile Czech Republic France Greece
Guatemala Hungary Italy Japan Poland Portugal Singapore
South Korea Switzerland Thailand Turkey Ukraine Vietnam

Oxford is a registered trademark of Oxford University Press
in the UK and in certain other countries.

Published in India
by Oxford University Press, New Delhi

© Oxford University Press 2008

The moral rights of the author have been asserted
Database right Oxford University Press (maker)

First published 2008

ISBN-13: 978-0-19-569373-7
ISBN-10: 0-19-569373-6

The publishers, series editor, and authors can accept no responsibility
for any loss or inconvenience caused by any error or misinformation
in the series, though every care is taken in compiling the books.

Typeset in Goudy 11/13.2
by Eleven Arts, Keshav Puram, Delhi 110 035
Printed in India by Rajshree Photolithographers, Delhi 110 032
Published by Oxford University Press
YMCA Library Building, Jai Singh Road, New Delhi 110 001

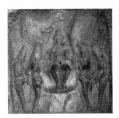

Series Editor's Preface

There are 851 sites on the World Heritage List, as on June 2007, 'inscribed' as properties by the World Heritage Committee of United Nations Educational, Scientific and Cultural Organization (UNESCO). The list includes: 660 cultural, 166 natural, and 25 mixed sites in 141 States Parties. These are 'considered to be of outstanding value to humanity', and belong to all mankind. The preservation of this shared heritage concerns all of us. India is an active member-state on the World Heritage Forum since 1977, and is one of the countries on the list, with 27 World Heritage Sites. Of these, 22 are recorded as cultural sites, while the rest are natural sites.

I am delighted that the Oxford University Press is publishing brief books on each of the 22 cultural sites, under its series titled Monumental Legacy. So far, the following cultural sites of India have been listed as World Heritage Sites:

Ajanta Caves (1983), Ellora Caves (1983), Agra Fort (1983), Taj Mahal (1983), Sun Temple, Konark (1984), Group of Monuments at Mahabalipuram (1985), Churches and Convents of Goa (1986), Group of Monuments at Khajuraho (1986), Group of Monuments at Hampi (1986), Fatehpur Sikri (1986), Group of Monuments at

Pattadakal (1987), Elephanta Caves (1987), Brihadisvara Temple, Thanjavur (1987), extended to include under 'Great Living Chola Temples', Gangaikondacholapuram and Darasuram (2004), Buddhist Monuments at Sanchi (1989), Humayun's Tomb (1993), Qutb Minar and its Monuments (1993), the Darjeeling Himalayan Railway (1999) extended to include under 'Mountain Railways of India', the Nilgiri Mountain Railway (2005), Bodh Gaya (2002), Rock Shelters of Bhimbetka (2003), Champaner-Pavagadh Complex (2004), Chhatrapati Shivaji Terminus, formerly Victoria Terminus (2004), and the Red Fort Complex (2007).

There is scope, indeed, for recognition of many more Indian sites in future on the World Heritage List. I am sure that as, and when, these are declared as World Heritage Sites, they will be included under the Monumental Legacy series of the Oxford University Press.

The Oxford University Press, in consultation with me, has invited the experts in the field to contribute small books, addressed to general readers, on each of these 22 World Heritage Cultural Sites in India. These books obviously differ from cheap tourist books and glossy guide books and, at the same time, also from specialized monographs. Their importance lies in the fact that they are written by authorities on the subject to enable visitors to see the monuments in proper perspective.

My sincere thanks to all the authors of the Series and to the editorial staff at Oxford University Press. Their constant support and enthusiasm is much appreciated.

Devangana Desai

Contents

Illustrations

Figures

Photos

Plates

Acknowledgements

Photos and Plates

Mohan Nagaswamy and Vishnu Mohan

Figures

I–IX, Archaeological Survey of India, New Delhi
III–IX American Institute of Indian Studies, Gurgaon

Preface and Acknowledgements

Mamallapuram situated on the seashore is essentially an ocean of artistic aspiration of a Pallava king, Rajasimha (700 CE) who called himself an 'Ocean of Arts', *kala samudrah*. He was no doubt steeped in Indian religious ethos, myths and legends, music and dance and all the finer things in life. To express them he assumed different titles that are found engraved at Mamallapuram and Kanchipuram. But it was his creative genius in the field of poetry—both visual and verbal (*drsya kavya* and *sravya kavya*) that exemplified in his sculptural art. I have had the good fortune of studying this magnificent group of monuments for the past fifty years and more in the company of most outstanding scholars like A.L. Basham, C. Sivaramamurthi, K.R. Sreenivasan and others and also a galaxy of renowned dignitaries from all parts of the world both in my official and private capacity. I was always stunned by the spontaneous response from viewers of these creations. They invariably said, 'No doubt these are world class art creations'. As a student of classical Sanskrit, the inscriptions on the monuments also fascinated me by their beauty and suggestions that speak of Rajasimha's love of poetry, arts, music, and dance.

I was overjoyed when the Oxford University Press invited me to write a book on this World Heritage Site as a part of Monumental Legacy series. I express my profound thanks to the editors at the Press for the successful fruition of this venture. It was Devangana Desai who first suggested that I should write on this site and encouraged me to undertake this work and also made valuable editorial suggestions that I cherish very much and am beholden to her for this opportunity. All the photographs used in this work barring two were specially taken by my son Mohan Nagaswamy and grandson Vishnu Mohan with understanding and devotion they deserve appreciation. The Director General of Archaeological Survey of India and Director General of the American Institute of Indian Studies have very kindly accorded permission to reproduce some of the drawings and plans in this work for which I am grateful to them

The book I am sure would be read with keen interest by students and professors as well as visitors to the site.

Introduction

Mamallapuram is the ancient name of the town Mahabalipuram on the coast of Tamil Nadu. The name is derived from the word 'Mallal' which means prosperity in Tamil. Once upon a time backwaters entered deep into the township at its western end. This natural advantage enabled Mamallapuram to allow heavy boats as well as small ships laden with goods to enter and anchor on its shores. There are several allusions in early Tamil literature to the overseas trade and prosperous commerciality of the town where ships entered and left the port with commodities.

According to a legend, it was only in the sixteenth century that the name of the town changed to Mahabalipuram, after the name of the demon king Mahabali who in the Vamana *avatara*, dwarf incarnation of Lord Vishnu, gifted three steps of land to the Lord in his cosmic form.

Mamallapuram seems to have been an important centre for the Cholas who ruled during the early mediaval period (*c.* 850–1279). Salt production was a royal prerogative in ancient times. Some of the large salt pans used for manufacturing salt from sea water, both in the north and south of Mamallapuram, bear the names of the ruling Chola monarchs. Salt production was an important activity in Mamallapuram as can be seen from an inscription which refers to an 'Alam' meaning salt pan in the village. The ancient port town was mainly connected to the Pallava capital Kanchipuram. Kanchipuram was the most important city in the northern part of Tamil Nadu for over two thousand years, before the seventeenth century, when Madraspattanam (modern Madras, now renamed Chennai) began assuming importance with the advent of the British East India Company. Mamallapuram was connected to Kanchipuram by two routes, one the inland route, via Thirumukkudal and Thirukkalukkundram, and the second by a waterway. The River Palaru, which skirted Kanchipuram, reaches the Bay of Bengal at a place called Vayalur, about ten kilometres south of Mamallapuram. So, one can reach Mamallapuram easily through this route.

Pallava monuments, especially of Rajasimha, the creator of the monuments, are to be found on both the routes from Kanchi. At Thirukalukkundram there is a lofty Hill of Vultures with a Pallava temple built on top of the hill. Nearby is a place Vallam, where two excavated cave temples of Mahendra Varman I, c. 600 CE are found. At Vayalur, there is an old Shiva temple, which has a Pallava pillar built at the entrance gateway listing fifty-four generations of Pallava rulers, beginning from mythical Brahma down to the reign of Rajasimha. It has been suggested that this pillar was intended to perpetuate the coronation of Rajasimha. Mamallapuram's trade connection with the Pallava capital ought to have enhanced its prosperity.

Around the fifth–sixth centuries, Vaishnava saint Bhutattalvar was born at Mamallapuram. He is considered to be one among the three early Vaishnava saints (Mudal-Alvar-Muvar). The character of the town, which was essentially a commercial town since its foundation, now changed into a religious one as it soon became a sacred centre of pilgrimage. Bhutattalvar has sung about different Vaishnava settlements in the South as well as Mamallapuram.

Around the middle of the seventh century (650 CE), the then Pallava ruler Narasimha Varman I, sent a successful naval expedition to Sri Lanka, in order to help his friend Manavarman regain his lost throne. Narasimha Pallava, who had the title 'Mamalla', was supposed to have sent his naval fleet from this port town, which he renamed as Mamallapuram. Though it became a pilgrim centre, it also continued to remain a commercial town as is denoted by the term 'puram'. Though Mamalla's name is associated with this town no artistic activity of either Mamalla, or his illustrious father Mahendra I, is noticed here. There is also no record of his successors till the reign of Rajasimha around 690 CE. But from about 690, for nearly forty years, the town changed its garb and was teaming with artists, and visits of the king, his queens, and retinue, who swarmed the place to see the magnificent creations. The place seemed to come alive with art and artists. The puranic legends, that had long filled the hearts of people through oral traditions, suddenly sprang into visual forms to the delight of the onlookers. The charming legend of Krishna lifting the Govardhana Hill, to provide shelter to the cowherds, to save them from the torrential rain let lose by Indra the king of gods; the story of Arjuna, one of the heros of Mahabharata, doing severe penance on the slopes of the Himalayas beside the river Ganga to obtain Pashupata *astra*, a weapon from Lord Shiva, with celestials and terrestrial thronging to the site to have a glimpse of this extraordinary scene; the legend of the great victory attained by the Goddess Durga over the arrogant buffalo-headed demon, Mahishasura; the tale of Vishnu assuming the form of a wild boar, Varaha and plunging into the ocean to bring the submerged goddess, Mother Earth; Vishnu taking three strides to subdue the demon-king Mahabali; and that of the charming Goddess Lakshmi, personification of beauty and feminine tenderness—all these familiar legends sprang alive, casting a spell of wonder and admiration. The incessant sound of chisels, the majesty of the king's retinue, the movement of hovering horses, and the excited chattering of people must have undoubtedly made Mamallapuram a wonderland.

The joy that permeated the town for nearly forty years came to a sudden end when Rajasimha died. The sound of the chisels ceased. The king's retinue hurriedly rushed to Kanchipuram, never to return. Work on numerous monuments, that had been initiated simultaneously, was left unfinished. The king's dream of bringing to life his aesthetic subjects remained a dream and could not be transformed into reality. The glorious Pallava dynasty started tottering. The young twelve-year old king who succeeded had to run for his life from the onslaught of his enemies. He came back only to be driven out again, and then imprisoned. It was a struggle for a long rule marked by frequent clashes and disturbances. Since art springs in serenity, Mamallapuram lost it for ever with the loss of political stability. 730 CE marked the date of artistic collapse in Mamallapuram.

ONE

Artists and their Material

T
he world is beholden to the artists who worked under the
Pallavas for the creation of such exquisite monumental art
at Mamallapuram. The question that naturally arises is whether
the name of any of the artists who worked at this site is known. 'The
names of indigenous artists are generally not known and there are
suggestions that even mentioning their names was taboo. Most often
the artists did not receive due recognition at the hands of their patrons.'
This view, however, is not based on available records and seems to be
a preconceived notion, for the names of some of the leading artists
who worked at Mamallapuram are still preserved in inscriptions.

On the western outskirts of Mamallapuram, a little less than a
kilometre away, on the high road is a hamlet of Mamallapuram now
called Puncheri. There are rock boulders here, among which is a
low rock with a cavity that is called 'Horse cistern of lame Virappan'.
On the periphery of this rock are seven labels written in old Tamil
and Grantha script—Catamukhyan, Kalyani, Kevada-Perumtaccan,
Kollan Seman, Kuna-mallan, Namah-Thiruvorriyur Abhajan, Payyam
Ilippan. All these are personal names but they undoubtedly indicate
that they were artists. The name Kevada Perumtaccan, for example,
is the name given to a great artist. The name, in Tamil, consists of
three parts: Kevada is a personal name, *perum* means great in Tamil,

and *taccan* means sculptor. Taccan is a Prakrit form of the Sanskirt word *takshaka*, denoting sculptor. Master sculptors and artists were themselves architects who were mentioned in many inscriptions as Perumtaccan. There are pointed references to great architects and sculptors as Perumtaccan in sixth–eighth century epigraphical records. Many such examples could be cited which demonstrates the respected position given to the sculptors and artists in Tamil Nadu.

It would be interesting to give a brief account of the Mamallapuram artists before we proceed to further examine these names. Several royal charters of the Pallava and Pandya kings have survived, which show the artists/sculptors were held in great esteem. They were very close to the king and were trusted secret scribes (*rahasyadhikrit*) of the king. The king's charters show that the scribes were conferred royal titles and were mentioned as the writers of the charters. The Dharmashastras, prescribe that the name of the scribe should be written at the end of the document. When the kings made any gift of villages to learned brahmins, one share of the village was allotted to this sculptor/artist.

It is interesting to note that Kanchipuram was a great centre for artists. Many records of the Pallava age mention that these artists hailed from Kanchipuram. They seem to have had an effective guild, to which they referred to learn about their obligations. The name Perumtaccan, appearing in a part of Mamallapuram, shows they were working on these monuments. These artists/sculptors belonged to five groups, often calling themselves 'the five-artisan group'. This indicates that though they were all adept in sculpture, they occasionally divided themselves according to the material they worked with, such as stone, wood, iron, gold, and ivory. Early epigraphs of the Pallavas mention that all these sculptors/artists worked under the king as scribes. But these divisions were not so well marked. Another name occurring at Mamallapuram is Gunamalla, which seems to be a royal title conferred on the artist. These names, occurring at the suburb of Mamallapuram, denote that they were artisans. As these records are assignable to *c*. 700 they represent the Mamallapuram artists. What needs to be borne in mind is the media through which they were expressing themselves.

A large number of rock shelters, dating from the second century, have been found in the Tamil countryside with neatly chiselled stone beds, bearing Tamil/Brahmi inscriptions. Many stones belonging to the same period and portraying images of heroes, with their names inscribed on them, have also come to light. These are carved on granite slabs, in low bas-relief, often in animated poses, pointing to the art of carving prevalent even at the village level. And yet it was brick and mortar, and perhaps wood, that was generally preferred for construction. Most of the temples were built of brick and mortar. The image in the sanctum was made of stucco, though some Shiva lingas made of stone were also installed. One of the earliest Shiva lingas in stone, assignable to second–first centuries BCE, is found at Gudimallam near the northern borders of Tamil Nadu. The preference for stucco or painting also continued. A technique that deserves attention was the art of carving sculptures on brick walls, and then covering them with lime plaster and paint. Such sculptures were chiselled on brick walls, after erecting the brick walls. This technique was later transferred to stone carving from the middle of the sixth century. With the introduction of a large number of cave temples, in which rocks were scooped to provide wall surfaces, chiselling sculptures came to dominate the scene. Simultaneously soft stone was used in place of brick to erect the wall structures and carved sculptures. Whether it was granite, sandstone or brick on which the sculptures were carved, all were plastered and painted at the end. Ultimately no difference between a stone temple or brick temple could be found. The artists' main technique remained carving large-scale sculptures.

The enormous labour involved in quarrying stones and transporting them to distant places was not prevalent. The rock cut caves and structural stone temples built of sandstone, found in Mamallapuram and Kanchi, stand witness to this trend. When Mahendra Varman I carved his first cave temple at Mandagappattu, he exclaimed about his novel technique of carving stone, stating that he dispensed with the use of brick, wood, metal, and stucco. Temples built of a single material like stone were called pure temples or shuddha type, while those using more than one material were called mixed or mishra variety. The engraving of rock cut temples and sculptures consumed less time than structural temples of granite. The medium of their creation being already present readily, the artists of Mamallapuram were freer to express themselves.

TWO

Authorship

E nthusiastic visitors to the fascinating monuments and sculptures at Mamallapuram are curious to know about the authors of these creations. This question has dominated the visitors' curiosity for the past three hundred years. This enquiry may be divided into two periods—prior to the discovery of the inscriptions around 1800 and the post-epigraphical phase. The first phase was based mainly on conjectures. As Mamallapuram has attracted connoisseurs for the past five hundred years, especially travellers and mariners, their acquaintance with art forms of other countries made them suggest that these were either created by Chinese artists or were the works of Thai artists or they were the works of Buddhists. The Chinese source arose from the Tiger cave which depicted the Yali heads that resembled dragons. Travellers who had seen Buddhist stupas asserted that they were the creations of Buddhist faith.

These suggestions gradually faded into oblivion when the inscriptions began pointing to a local dynasty—the Pallavas. As more royal records emerged, they gave rise to a fairly recognizable framework within which these creations could be accommodated. Names of some powerful Pallava rulers became known. Among them Mahendra Varman, Mamalla Narasimha Varman, Parameshvara Varman, and

Rajasimha, spanning about one hundred years from the seventh to the beginning of the eighth century CE are important. Mahendra I (590–630 CE) inscribed his titles on a few cave temples. These inscriptions also mention specifically his love for sculpture and painting and also for creating such novel temples. Rajasimha (690–728), expressed his fascination for art by calling himself 'Ocean of Art' (kala samudhrah) and he, too, built monuments at numerous places. Some of his names are found at the Mamallapuram monuments. Thus, the date of these monuments got narrowed down to the seventh and early-eighth century.

Apart from the inscriptions, a large number of articles and guides appeared between eighteenth and twentieth centuries, in which art historians tried to highlight stylistic differences between the various monuments. The volume of literature on style soon swelled. Writers were weighed down by stylistic considerations and assigned a chronological development to these monuments. This tendency went, at times, to an extreme level, even to the extent of alleging that some of the inscriptions were misappropriated.

Mahendra Varman I was an eminent poet and a lover of arts. Among his titles the following are well known: Chitra-kara-Puli, a tiger among artists; Chettakari, a builder of great temples; Vichitra-Chitta, one who is fascinated by rare and special arts, particularly sculpture, bas-relief, and paintings; and Sankirna-jati, one who could blend different classical forms. Mahendra created two great Sanskrit farcical plays that stand to this day as unique pieces, ridiculing the contemporary society, particularly the religious faiths that deserved condemnation. In one of the cave temples there is an inscription stating that he built the temple without the use of brick, mortar, metal, and wood. This led the scholars to believe that this was his first creation. Ananda Coomaraswamy, however, points out that Mahendra might have been inspired by the trend found in the Krishna Valley of Andhradesha. This suggestion seems probable keeping in mind that Mahendra assumed more Telugu titles than Sanskrit ones. There is a cave temple excavated by him at Pallavaram in Chennai that lists nearly seventy titles of Mahendra, out of which forty-seven are in Telugu. Similarly, the rock cut cave on top of Thiruchirappalli hill lists nearly one hundred titles of Mahendra, out of which seventy are in Telugu. Mahendra's association with Telugu country is more pronounced than that of his successors. The Telugu region had a long tradition of sculptural art, known from the Amaravati and Nagarjunakonda Buddhist stupas. There were also some excavated cave temples in the region. Obviously, Mahendra was inspired by this tradition which he brought to the Tamil country.

Mahendra's cave temples were simple excavations, the only sculptures being those of the *dvarapalas* carved on either side. One such remarkable cave is found at Thiruchirappalli, which has a monumental sculpture of Shiva as Gangadhara. Mahendra himself has eulogized this Gangadhara in a beautiful Sanskrit inscription. The simple technique of carving the pillar which was square at the bottom and top with an octagonal fluting in the middle was considered his peculiar style. The sanctum of his temples no longer house any deity, but originally there were either stucco or painted images enshrined. Though there are many cave excavations around Kanchi, Chennai, and Trichy, there is no monument by Mahendra at Mamallapuram, as no inscription by him is found there.

Narasimha Varman I, his son and successor (630–668 CE) was a great fighter and so he assumed the title 'Maha-malla', the great fighter. From his records and subsequent Pallava epigraphs, it is seen that he chased the Chalukya ruler Pulakeshi from the outskirts of Kanchi to Vatapi, the Chalukya capital, engaged him in a battle, killed him, and gained a significant victory. He assumed the title Vatapi Konda, the conqueror of Vatapi, and occupied it for nearly thirteen years. His victory over Pulakeshi and the conquest of Vatapi are invariably mentioned in his inscriptions and in subsequent Pallava records. Some of the monuments at Mamallapuram are assigned, by some scholars, to Mamalla Narasimha I, on stylistic grounds. But since none of the inscriptions found at Mamallapuram refer to his conquest of Vatapi and victory over Pulakeshi no monument of Mamallapuram could be assigned to Narasimha I

Parameshvara Varman I, father of Rajasimha (670–690 CE) was the third Pallava king of some importance who ruled in the seventh century. He, too, had to fight the Chalukyas. In his royal charter he graphically describes his battle with the Chalukyas, where he defeated their ruler. He assumed the title Ranarasika Puramarddana, he who destroyed the capital of Ranarasika Vikramaditya Chalukya. However, as this outstanding achievement of Parameshvara is not mentioned in any inscription at Mamallapuram, it seems that none of the monuments could be ascribed to him.

This brings us to King Rajasimha who, by all accounts, is considered to be the author of all the monuments at Mamallapuram. According to his inscriptions he is said to have spent all his wealth on temples (Deva-Brahmana-Satkrita-Atma Vibhavah). In all his known inscriptions, one of his most significant titles—Atyanta-kama, one who has endless desires or fascination, is mentioned. Many of the monuments at Mamallapuram not only bear this title but are also named as Atyanta-kama–Pallaveshvara-griham, the Ishvara temple of Atyanta-kama. Such monuments at Mamallapuram include two cave temples and two monoliths. Further, these monuments carry inscriptions that are specifically foundation inscriptions, declaring that they were his creations (*tena idam karitam*). His another significant title found in the records is Kala Samudrah, Ocean of Arts. His love for variety, visible in the construction of different types of temples, in the employment of different scripts, and in different styles of expression is clearly evident in these monuments. It would indeed be interesting to know the personality of the patron of these monuments.

THREE

Rajasimha, the Builder

Mamallapuram was probably established as a port by Narasimha I after his title 'Mamalla'. However, there is no specific evidence to connect this association. But, it seems that all the monuments were created by Rajasimha who was more popular among his subjects as 'Mamalla' (*Vidita Mahamalla sabdah prajanam*) as is shown in his inscription at Vayalur. Rajasimha's monuments are found at Kanchipuram, Panamalai, Vayalur, Thirupporur, Thirukkalukkundram, Dalavanur, and Mamallapuram, all in Pallava country, and also at Thiruppattur near Thiruchirappalli. There are excavated cave temples, rock cut monoliths, open air bas-reliefs, and structural temples. He employed variations in scripts, like simple Pallava Grantha, ornate Pallava Grantha, Grantha in which calligraphic letters resemble birds, animals, and reptiles, and finally simple and ornate Nagari script. Also, at different places he chose different modes of expression. For example, at Kanchi he arranged over three hundred of his titles in alphabetical order, writing each title in four different scripts. At Vayalur, he tabulated a list of fifty-four Pallava kings, beginning from the first-known king, arranged in order of succession, till his own times. Interestingly, this record begins at the bottom of a pillar, and goes up spirally. At Saluvankuppam, we have his authorship inscription, both in Grantha and Nagari script. Each of his known monuments is laid out differently in plan, elevation, and distribution of sculptures. His choice of the sites to build his monumental temples, on top of a hill at Panamalai, among the plain fields at Kanchipuram, and on the seashore at Mamallapuram, depicts his fascination for natural environments.

Rajasimha was born to Pallava Parameshvara, the conqueror of the Chalukya Ranarasika-Vikramaditya I. He resembled Guha-Subrahmanya, born from Parameshvara (Shiva). He calls Pallavas as pious princes who destroyed the pride of the evil dark age. According to him the Pallavas were supposed to be truthful, profoundly-learned princes who knew how to practise the *Trivarga*, who assiduously honoured aged people, subdued lust and other internal foes, excelled in the knowledge of weapons, and were mighty people endowed with polity and modesty. This illustrious king 'Atyanta-kama' was well known for his great statesmanship. Like Kama he charmed refined women in secret, like Indra he protected the followers of Vedic learning, like Lord Vishnu he protected sages from the onslaught of enemies, and like Kubera, the lord of wealth, he gifted all his wealth to good people.

He was probably named Narasimha II after his great grandfather and assumed the title Rajasimha upon coronation. He was proud of his race and was known as the 'Sun among the Pallavas', an ornament to his family, and Vrisha-dhvaja, virtually the fluttering flag of his family. He seems to have a uniquely beautiful personality (*ekasundara*, unequalled in beauty) and had a very pleasant appearance. Rajasimha's military prowess is evident from his various titles such as Aparajita (the Invincible), Ranajayah (conqueror of battles), Chakravarti (an emperor), and Dura-darshi (one with a vision). He always preferred the path of righteousness and followed the rules enjoined in ancient traditional treatises. Rajasimha was a great scholar who ruled according to the various branches of knowledge (*Shastra drishti*). He was endowed with active habits (*Nityotsaha*) and was an expert (*Upaya-Nipuna*) at handling things. He was also an accomplished musician, especially well-versed in playing stringed instruments, particularly the *vina*, and was compared to the great sage Narada. He had an outstanding personality among men and considered righteous conduct as his armour (*dharma-kavachah*). A lion among men, he called himself Kanchi Mahamanih, the crest jewel of the city of Kanchi. The long list of his titles begins with Rajasimha, Atyanta-kama, and Ranajaya. Thus, he himself has given importance to the title Atyanta-kama both in the verse referring to his birth, and also at the beginning of the list of his over three hundred titles. There are several titles that denote his passion for arts. One of his significant titles, kala samudrah reveals that he was obviously inspired by his illustrious predecessor Mahendra Varman, who styled himself as a tiger among artists. His title Mahendra-Parakramah (one who equalled Mahendra in his achievements) explicitly indicates this. His love of arts extended beyond sculptural art to music and dance, and is shown by titles such as Vadya Vidyadhara, celestial musician in playing instruments, Vina Narada and Atodya Tumburu, Sage Tumburu in playing musical instruments. His great fascination for the epics— Ramayana and Mahabharata (Itihasa-Priyah)—also suggests that he was fond of creating history. Rajasimha seems to have concentrated on increasing the greatness of his country (Desa-vardhanah).

In his religious leanings, particularly through temple-building and institutionalizing worship, he strictly followed the ritual treatises called Agamas. Atyanta-kama was a great devotee of Shiva, as is mentioned in each of his records. Titles like Ishana-sharanah, Devadeva bhaktah, and Ishvara bhaktah illustrate his Shiva bhakti. An oft-respected title denoting his Shaiva devotion is *Shiva chudamani*, one who bears Shiva as his crest jewel. The inscription at Vayalur states that he was Atyanta-kama, one with boundless desires in adoring the sacred feet of Lord Shambu for ever (*Shambhor padaravinda dvaya Paricarane nityam atyantakama*). True to this expression, most of his creations at Mamallapuram and elsewhere are dedicated to Shiva. But this devotion was not against the worship of Vishnu or other gods, as the extreme sectarian form of worship was unknown then. Rajasimha himself assumed the titles of Narasimha, Simha Vishnu, etc. By his time in 700 CE, the Agamic literature seems to have been well codified, for he declares that he was a follower of Agamas (*Agamanusari*) and took the Agamas as the authoritative and guiding principles (*Agama Pramanah*). He was the first ruler to declare that he followed the various teachings of *Shaiva-siddhanta marga* and got all his impurities cleaned according to it(*Vidita bahunayah Shaiva Siddhanta Marga*).

A study of the Mamallapuram monuments (Fig. I) in the context of these extraordinary qualities possessed by Rajasimha significantly alters the perception of these beautiful creations. The several caves, monoliths, open-air sculptures at Mamallapuram exhibit a unique creativity and innovation that differs from others found elsewhere. No two monuments at Mamallapuram are identical. They reflect the personality of a great art lover. The selection of different rocks and art forms suited to the natural formation of rocks stands out as one moves from one monument to another. The great desire to create so many structures simultaneously, by employing several artists at the same place, was no ordinary one. Hence, there was a sudden abandoning of work on all monuments when Rajasimha died. There was no one to continue his legacy.

Mamallapuram is the only place where the concept of art forms assumes primary importance and the religious and legendary themes play only a subsidiary role. The sculptors cut out monoliths, excavated temples in caves or open rocks, choosing the rocks on the basis of their natural formation—like Arjuna's penance on the banks of celestial Ganga, or the hill lifted by Krishna, or the location of Vishnu reclining right on the waves of the ocean on which he sleeps. They all portray an artistic sensitivity that does not follow a rigid textual grammar. Every curve and position of the sculptures vividly portrays a supremely elegant conception.

The linearity and spatiality of the figures carved in the rocks impart a fullness to them that captivates the onlooker's imagination. Every portrayal pulsates with the inner spirit of the theme that is portrayed. The monkey-group of figures—the male, female, and the young one, the male searching for lice on the female, which in turn feeds the young one is a supurb study. The great elephants—the male, female, and their calf wading through the woods to the river bank are an unforgettable portrayal. The cow that tenderly caresses its calf while a cowherd is milking her truly reflects the simpler character of each animal (Photo 1). In fact, the animal studies in Mamallapuram remain unparalleled (Photo 2) in Indian art. The monoliths, that is, the *rathas*, too, are unique, where each temple is

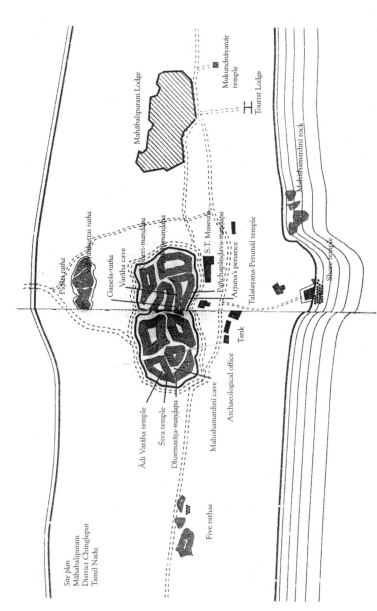

Fig. I: Site plan of Mahabalipuram, from latest guidebook of Archaeological Survey of India (hereafter ASI), 2006

Photo 1: Close-up of the cow and the calf, Govardhanadhari relief

Photo 2: A lovely deer

presented as a sculpture. The Mahishasura Mardini cave where the sculpture makes one feel the rage with which adamant demonic power is annihilated by the goddess Mahishasura Mardini, the feminine power par excellence. The legend is brilliantly brought to life in this depiction in stone.

We owe these stupendously beautiful creations to Rajasimha whose tremendous desire for variety, coupled with an extraordinary sense of aesthetic perception, created for us this exotic sensory wonderland.

Rajasimha's successor Nandivarman had to struggle throughout his long rule to hold on to his throne. Hence, no great monuments were created subsequently. He created a Vishnu temple at Kanchi, when some peace returned, but that was only a flicker of disappearing art. By the beginning of the eighth century the medium of construction had changed from soft sandstone to hard granite, resulting in sculptural art reaching a low ebb.

Currently there are two prominent theories about the authorship of the Mamallapuram monuments. One holds that on the basis of stylistic variation, three periods can be distinguished—Mahendra style, Mamalla style, and Rajasimha style. This theory holds that work at Mamallapuram was started by Narasimha I and continued by successive rulers till the end of Rajasimha's reign. This means that all the rulers from Mamalla's time took interest in these excavations, continued the work simultaneously on all the monuments, and with the death of Rajasimha all the monuments were left unfinished. The stylistic evolution is sought to be shown through the designs of pillars, deep or shallow carvings of the figures and some other peculiar features. This theory seems somewhat contradictory. As has been mentioned earlier, the most significant achievements of Mamalla, or Parameshvara, are not mentioned in any of the inscriptions here. Nor is their interest in excavating monuments hinted. Also, as most of these monuments are unfinished, any attempt to distinguish style within a period of about fifty years is fraught with difficulty.

The other theory is that all the monuments were the creations of one king, namely Rajasimha. This theory is based on the unimpeachable evidence of inscriptions, which consist of foundation records, claiming that they were made by the king Rajasimha. Many records found in different monuments are repetitions of the records of the same king. The theory is also based on the study of Rajasimha's extraordinary personality. The Mamallapuram creations are first and foremost artistic expressions of his passions and religious fervour is only secondary. A frequently asked question is, whether it would have been possible for one king to create so many monuments in his own lifetime. As has been earlier pointed, quarrying, transporting, dressing, and chiselling of stone would have been more time consuming than carving as is the case here. Illustrious monarchs, like Rajaraja Chola and Krishnadeva, built more monuments in a much shorter time. It is not an impossible task. But what is of utmost importance is the occurrence of foundation inscriptions referring to their creation. If these foundation records are set aside, one will have no way of dating any monument. And lastly, to say that the earlier monuments had been misappropriated by the later king, who inscribed his record on them, would amount to imputing dishonesty to a great artist; nor can one justify by any means such a blasphemous claim. That all these monuments are the creations of a single king with an extraordinary aesthetic perception is a fact.

FOUR

List of Monuments

Cave Temples (13)

1. Adivaraha cave
2. Atinanachanda cave
3. Dharmaraja mandapa
4. Koneri mandapa
5. Kotikkal mandapa
6. Mahishasura Mardini cave
7. Mahisha cave
8. Pancha Pandava cave temple
9. Pulippudar mandapa
10. Ramanuja mandapa
11. Tiger cave
12. Trimurti cave
13. Varaha cave
14. Unfinished mandapa

Rathas (10)

1. Draupadi ratha
2. Arjuna ratha

3. Bhima ratha
4. Dharmaraja ratha
5. Sahadeva ratha
6. Ganesha ratha
7. Valayankuttai ratha
8. Pidari rathas (2)
9. Unfinished ratha

Bas-reliefs (8)

1. Arjuna's penance
2. Elephant peacock monkey group
3. Horse group
4. Krishna govardhanadhari mandapa
5. Lion with Durga
6. Miniature Yalimandapa
7. Unfinished Arjuna's penance
8. Diving Varaha

Structural Temples (4)

1. Seashore temple
2. Olakkanneshvara temple
3. Mukunda Nayanar temple
4. Central temple of Vishnu
5. Kali
6. Lion seat

FIVE

Monuments

Cave Temples

Adivaraha Cave

One of the best preserved but least visited cave temples in Mamallapuram (Fig. II) is the Adivaraha cave temple, situated in the west of the village near the Mahishasura Mardini cave. This temple has been under continuous worship from almost 700 CE, and is generally kept locked except in the mornings and evenings during worship. For the rest of the day the key remains with the priest living in the village. He can be approached by the visitors with a request to open the temple. The cave is not visited very often as an unimpressive stone pavilion, built in the sixteenth century obscures the view of the cave temple. The temple is dedicated to Lord Vishnu, in his third incarnation as Varaha, lifting Goddess Earth from the depths of the ocean. The form of Varaha emerging from the oceanic waters with the goddess is called Adi-Varaha, the Primordial Boar, and hence the name, Adivaraha cave.

The cave temple scooped out in the rock faces west. The innermost sanctum carries a stucco image of Varaha with the goddess

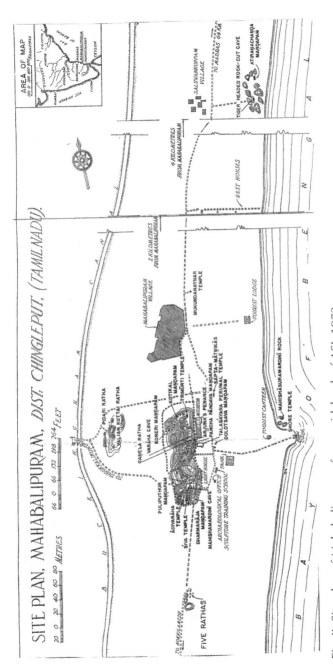

Fig. II: Site plan of Mahabalipuram, from guidebook of ASI, 1972

Earth. He has four arms and holds the conch and the discus, with his rear arms and the Earth goddess with his front arms. The Pallava features of the image are not discernible as the whole image was plastered and painted in the sixteenth century. Unlike the Varaha sculpture in the Varaha cave, this image in the sanctum has no accompanying figures.

The sanctum has a small projection generally known as *ardha mandapa*, whose façade is adorned with sculptures of a pair of dvarapalas flanking the entrance in delightful profiles. Beyond them on either side are standing figures, one on the south representing the composite form of Shiva and Vishnu as Harihara, and the other Adishesha Nagaraja, standing beneath a five-hooded cobra.

The front mandapa pavilion, also rock cut, is in two bays. The front end is supported by two rock cut pillars that are now enmeshed by a wall. The other, interior pillars are supported by seated lions. In line with the sanctum are lateral bays, one on either side, housing extraordinarily graceful sculptures of Durga in the south and Lakshmi in the north, both carved on the rock face. These two lovely sculptures were covered with plaster. Like the Mahishasura Mardini sculpture, these two may be mentioned as being the acme of Mamallai art. The flowing lines, the volume, the flexions of the body, and the profiles of these images are at once arresting.

Eight-armed Durga on the left wall stands on the head of a buffalo, holding a conch and discus, bow and arrow, sword and shield in the three rear arms while the front arm is relaxed. The goddess has an oval face with an impressive headgear culminating in a lotus bud. On either side of the goddess are two guardian women, one wielding a bow and arrow and the other a sword and shield. At the feet of the goddess are devotees, one on either side, one in the pose of adoration and the other offering a lotus. At the upper level is a prancing lion to the left of the goddess, and to her right is an antelope, both being her mounts. There are several sculptures of Durga portrayed in Pallava monuments but there is none equal in its aesthetic appeal to this supremely elegant portrayal.

Vying with Durga is Lakshmi, on the northern lateral wall. The goddess is seated on a prominent lotus seat, holding a lotus in each arm. Lakshmi, true to her description in all literature and musical compositions is a picture of perfect beauty with a captivating face. She is flanked by two maidens on either side. At the top of the panel are two royal elephants, one on either side, one pouring water over the goddess, and the other ready to follow. The composition of the panel, with a masterly distribution of space and volume, singles out the Pallava sculptors as master sculptors.

The side walls of the front mandapa carry a standing figure of Shiva as Gangadhara in the north, and Brahma, the Creator, in the south. The sharp divide between Shaivism and Vaishnavism was not prevalent in early times. The trinity of Brahma, Vishnu, and Shiva shared equal prominence. The layout and distribution of the deities in this temple conform to the Vaishnava Agamic text, *Marichi Samhita*, which says that Durga, Lakshmi, Brahma, and Gangadhara should be placed to the right and left of the sanctum of Vishnu.

The cave temple has two almost life-size portraits of Pallava rulers which present remarkable studies in human portraits. On the south wall of the inner bay of the mandapa, is a standing king, pointing excitedly to the sanctum (Photo 3). He is accompanied by two of his queens draped in diaphanous lower garments. Immediately above the panel is an inscribed label, in Pallava Grantha characters, mentioning on the lintel the name of the king as Mahendra Potradhirajan. On the northern wall, opposite the above panel, is another group of portraits, depicting a king, seated majestically on a high seat. He is flanked by two women, one on each side, evidently his queens, all portrayed in life-size. Both the kings wear ordinary crowns. The figures are charming and majestic. Above the seated king is a label inscription on the lintel, reading Simhavishnu–Potradhirajan. As the name Potradhirajan is used in many inscriptions of the seventh–eighth centuries for the kings of the Pallava dynasty, it is undoubtedly clear that the Pallava rulers were responsible for not only this cave temple, but also other monuments of Mamallapuram. There are differences of opinion among scholars about the identity of the kings portrayed. The latest view, based on the study of inscriptions at Mamallapuram and Kanchipuram, is that the seated king is Rajasimha Pallava, who had the title Narasimha Vishnu. The other standing king is his son Mahendra III. Rajasimha and his son jointly built temples at Kanchi and other places, as at the Kailashanatha temple, where the main

Photo 3: Portrait of Mahendra Pallava III, the son of Rajasimha, the creator of Mahabalipuram monuments in the Adivaraha cave

temple was built by Rajasimha, and the other, immediately in front
at the entrance, was built by Mahendra. It is evident from the
inscription that Mahendra III built it along with his father.
The cave temple was originally decorated with a row of miniature
towers, or *shikharas*, on the façade. These may be seen even now.
Besides the unique portrayal of Pallava portraits and label inscriptions,
there are three inscriptions in the temple that highlight three aspects
of temple and culture.

The lintel in front of the sanctum, above the Harihara image,
is a Pallava inscription in Sanskrit, listing the ten incarnations of
Vishnu in order as Matsya (Fish), Kurma (Turtle), Varaha (Boar),
Narasimha (Man-lion), Vamana (Dwarf), Rama (Parashurama),
Rama (Raghurama), Rama (Balarama), Buddha, and Kalki. This
inscription can be ascribed to 700 CE, by which time Buddha was
accepted as the ninth avatar of Vishnu.

The second long inscription is in large Pallava Grantha characters,
inscribed on the floor in front of the sanctum, slightly to the south
of the centre, extolling the greatness of Rudra and the need to adore
him. This inscription, recording the greatness of Rudra or Shiva in a
Vishnu temple, is justified as varaha, is identified with Rudra in the
earliest poem of *Rig Veda*. It needs to be reiterated that the division
between Vaishnavism and Shaivism was, as yet, unknown. This was
still the Puranic religion with no bias whatsoever.

The third epigraphical record in Tamil was inscribed on the rocky
wall outside the temple, during the time of the Chola Rajendra II in
the middle of eleventh century CE. The name of this temple is recorded
here as Parameshvara-Mahavaraha-Vishnu griham. This is evidently
the name given by the original Pallava patron. Another inscription
here, by the same king, records the gifts made to this temple.

A sixteenth century inscription on the wall of the later mandapa
of the temple reveals that the temple conducted annual festivals, when
a bronze image of the god was taken out in procession. Endowment
was also made to enable the villagers to take the deity in procession,
during the festival, to the nearby hamlet of Puncheri, about one
mile away from Mamallapuram.

The simple and functional front mandapa, supported by pillars, was constructed in the sixteenth century, probably at the time when the front mandapa of Krishna Govardhanadhari in the centre of the village was also built.

Atiranachanda Cave

Saluvankuppam, a small village on the outskrits of Mamallapuram, about three kilometres to the north, was earlier known as Thiru Eluccil, that is a sacred centre for bringing deities in procession. It is more famous now by the name of Tiger cave, due to a fanciful cave temple with a row of Yali heads, carved in a semi-circular fashion like a *prabha-mandala*, that attracts numerous visitors. There is another cave temple at this site, a simple rock cut temple, a furlong to the north of it. The latter is important on account of its inscriptions. Further, about three hundred yards north-east, nearer to the shore, is a rock where a brick temple was erected in Pallava times with inscriptions calling it a Subrahmanya temple. The inscriptions were discovered at the beginning of twentieth century, and the remains of the brick temple have been uncovered only recently.

The label inscription on the central beam of the façade mentions this cave temple as the Atiranachanda-ishvara griha, evidently named after Atiranachanda Pallava, a title found for Rajasimha in Kanchipuram, Panamalai, Thirupporur, Vayalur, Mamallapuram, and the shore temples. Besides this, there are two inscriptions on the side walls of the cave. Interestingly, both inscriptions are identical and record that the temple was built by Rajasimha. The inscriptions give the titles of Atyanta-kama, Ranajaya, Shribhara, Chitra-karmukha, and Atiranachanda. K.R. Sreenivasan, too, mentions that this temple was excavated by Rajasimha.

Atiranachanda is a rectangular cave with simple pillars, having a central sanctum shrine excavated in the rear wall. The back wall of this sanctum contains a carved, panelled sculpture, depicting Somaskanda, Shiva, and Parvati seated on a common pedestal, with the child Skanda seated on the mother's lap. At the back are shown Brahma and Vishnu, to the right and left of Shiva, both adoring Somaskanda. In the centre of the sanctum is a fluted linga with sixteen facets. A linga-pitha made of a single stone appears to have slid from the top of the linga and is positioned at about half the linga's height. The circular lower part of the linga-pitha is missing. The highly polished black granite of the linga and the linga-pitha looks like basalt. The upper part of the linga, called the *puja-bhaga*, has incised lines which culminate in a flame-like form. These images were probably visualized as *jyotir-linga* 'symbol of flame' and do not suggest the phallus. The presence of Somaskanda, with Brahma and Vishnu adoring Shiva in his linga form recalls the Siddhantic view of the main deity.

Flanking the sanctum are carved dvarapalas. The side lateral walls are also carved with semi-finished Somaskanda images in the centre. A single row of pillars accommodates one bay of the temple. On the façade there are rectangular slots cut at regular intervals. Slots are also cut on the floor in front of the pillars in order to insert them. This may be an indication of an intention to add a structural pavilion in the front.

The two Sanskrit inscriptions are copies of the same record in two different contemporary scripts (Pallava Grantha and Nagari). According to them the cave temple was excavated by Atiranachanda as the abode of Shiva, Uma, Skanda, and the *ganas*. The Pallava Grantha inscription (Photo 4), in seventeen lines, is on the southern flank of the cutting in front of the façade, while the sixteen-line Nagari one is on the northern flank. While the principal verses are common to both, there is an additional seventh verse in the Pallava Grantha version, eulogizing the musical talents of the composer Kalakala, which is incidentally a surname of Rajasimha himself. Of these, the first and second verses are identical with the eighth and ninth verses of Atyanta-kama in his inscription in the Dharmaraja mandapam and Ganesha ratha.

The other surnames of the king, besides Atiranachanda, Shrinidhi, Kamaraja, Shribhara, Dhananjaya, and Sangrama dhira, are also found. Since most of these names are also used for Rajasimha in his Kanchipuram inscriptions, this inscription too must be attributed to him. A point of interest here is the earliest epigraphical reference to Bharata, the author of *Natya-Shastra*, in this inscription.

In front of this cave temple is a low rocky outcrop, like a stone plank on which is carved a lovely scene of Mahisahasura mardini,

Photo 4: Rajasimha's inscription in Atiranachanda cave referring to the authorship of the cave temple

annihilating the buffalo headed demon who is running for his life in haste, unable to bear the onslaught of the lion mount of the goddess, with his hand behind his back and begging for mercy with the other. It is a good example of Mamallapuram artist creating something purely out of artistic instinct that has no requirement for ritual purpose.

Dharmaraja Mandapa

As one approaches the Mahishasura Mardini cave from Arjuna's Penance, this simple cave temple is visible. It faces east and is carved in two bays, with two massive pillars in the front and two at the back, all being square at the top and bottom and octagonal in the middle. A sanctum is carved in the centre in the back wall but no sculpture is found inside the sanctum. The central sanctum is projected in the front. Flanking the entrance of the sanctum are two carved dvarapalas, one on either side. Unfortunately both these sculptures were chiselled away during the Vaishnava resurgence.

Two more shrines were carved on either side of the central sanctum but the three are somewhat recessed into the back wall. All three are provided with steps. These three cells were probably dedicated to Brahma, Shiva, and Vishnu. The dedicatory inscription found in this cave is a repetition of the ones found in the Adivaraha cave, the Ramanuja mandapa, and the Ganesha ratha. The inscription names the temple as Atyantakama-Pallaveshvara-griham, that is, the Shiva temple of Atyanta-kama Pallava. Hence, this cave temple is clearly a creation of Rajasimha. The central shrine does not have any niche for Somaskanda or a socket to house a linga. This cave temple has been ascribed to the early phase of Parameshvara Varman I. But there does not seem to be any logical ground to attribute this to anyone other than Rajasimha. Its foundation inscription leaves its authorship in no doubt.

Koneri Mandapa

This cave temple of simple rectangular design with two bays is found in the middle of the western face of the rock. It contains seated-lion pillars outside and simple, slim, faceted pillars inside. There are five sanctums without any sculptures scooped in the wall. But all the sanctums contain a pedestal carved on the back wall suggesting that the deities were probably to be made of stucco and painted. It deserves to be noted that it was intended for five Shaiva deities. Three cells project forward while the other two are recessed. All the cells are rectangular in plan, have sockets on the floor to house the lingas, and there are five pairs of dvarapalas flanking each shrine. The two dvarapalas of the northern cells are unfortunately chipped off. From a study of the dvarapalas it seems that all the five cells were to be dedicated to Shiva in his five forms as Tatpurusha, Aghora, Sadyojata, Vamadeva, and Ishana. This is indicated by the two dvarapalas who have horn-like crowns on their heads. Those found in cells two and three are images of Nandikeshvara, the dvarapala of Shiva's sanctum. The dvarapalas guarding the fourth cell seem to show a fierce look and countenance, suggesting that the cell was to be dedicated to the Aghora form of Shiva. As this is a west-facing temple it is not unlikely that the main temple was dedicated to the Sadyojata form of Shiva.

As the temple bears no inscription and is attributed to the early period of Mamallapuram purely on a subjective basis, this view needs to be revised.

Kotikkal Mandapa

At the northern end of the main hillock is a rock cut cave temple facing west, with a sanctum scooped at the back. The sanctum is plain, without any carving or figures, but its façade has two female guardians, one holding a bow and the other a sword and shield. The presence of these two female doorkeepers indicates that the cave was dedicated to Goddess Durga.

Mahishasura Mardini Cave

This cave temple is famous for its breathtaking Mahishasura Mardini sculpture (Plate I). The cave is near the present lighthouse and faces east. The outer façade presents a simple, cave-like appearance, with fluted pillars. The central sanctum, preceded by a mandapa, enshrines a Somaskanda Shiva. It is carved at the back wall and is flanked on either side by two scooped-out shrines.

The two side wings of the front hall, contain two masterpieces of Pallava art. The north wall depicts the fight of Mahishasura Mardini with the buffalo-headed demon, and on the south is Lord Vishnu in his cosmic sleep (*Yoganidra*) on his serpent couch. Both the sculptures occupy the two walls from ground level to the ceiling. A perfect frame of wall is left out to picturize these great compositions.

The Mahishasura Mardini panel, after which the cave is named, is a supremely elegant creation. Historians have spontaneously described the beauty of this panel. It looks as though the artist conceived this side wall as a tightly-held canvas, framed perfectly, to picturize the episode with a central line drawn vertically to distribute the central characters. To the left is the march of Goddess Durga mounted on her prancing lion and carrying weapons in her hands. She is accompanied by a retinue holding weapons like swords, bows, and arrows. The retinue of the goddess consists of poised women and dwarfish big-bellied ganas. It presents a picture of female power strong enough to annihilate the arrogant and brutal manly power portrayed by the buffalo-headed demon, Mahishasura, opposing the goddess. It appears as if the little dwarfish ganas are sufficient for wiping out brute force. Symbolizing the striking power of virtue over vice is Goddess Durga on her powerful mount charging towards the asura. Her militant and aggressive posture suggests her skill in using weapons. The long sword in her right hand is the weapon she uses to sever the head of the demon.

To the right are shown Mahishasura and his soldiers in retreat. Mahishasura is already falling down as his left leg trembles to support his body. His big mace (*gada*) looks heavy in his hand. What seems to hold him up is his adamant nature and arrogant unwillingness to yield. One of his attendants in front has fallen dead, another cut into two pieces is shown falling head down, a poor third one is looking up pathetically, hiding himself behind the person in front and hoping to escape. The asura's trusted commander has retreated in shame and another has turned his back to the battlefield, looking back with meloncholy eyes seeking a route to escape. The scene is a brilliant exposition of evil routed by divine power. In India feminine power is worshipped by the Trinity—Brahma, Vishnu, and Shiva. In this panel it is glorified to perfection. This unparalled creation indeed justifies the Pallavas' greatness as sculptors.

On the opposite wall, two-armed Vishnu lies in a relaxed pose, head eastwards and legs extended to the west, with his face turned upwards. He wears a cylindrical crown and his eyes are closed in deep sleep. The ever-watchful five-hooded serpent, Ananta, spread out like an umbrella over his head, stands guard. The two demons, Madhu and Kaitabha, approach the foot of the Lord to attack him with clubs in their hands, but the cobra hisses, sending out waves of flames, and drives the demons away. The blazing flames following the asuras can be seen on the back wall. The frightened demons try to flee but the heat of the flames burns their backs. Two more figures are shown in the upper part of the panel, one a dwarfish manly figure and the other female, both flying joyfully to crush the demons. The dwarfish figure is the personification of Vishnu's weapon, the conch Panchajanya that loudly announces the victory over the demon. The female figure striking the demon is a personification of Vishnu's gada Kaumodaki.

Beneath the reclining Vishnu are three figures personifying Vishnu's *chakra* (discus, shown here with a crown on its head), Vishnu's mount, Vainateya Garuda (the eagle), and Bhudevi (the goddess Earth)with folded hands bent in adoration. Seated behind her is Sage Markandeya praising Vishnu for imparting an immortal message.

Inside the central sanctum is an imposing, majestic figure of Shiva seated on a throne, accompanied by his consort Parvati with the playful Skanda seated on her lap. Beneath their seat rests Shiva's mount, Nandi, fairly powerful and robust bull. The panel also depicts Vishnu and Brahma, at the top, adoring Shiva.

Mahisha Cave

The Tiger cave/Yali mandapa must be studied in association with another cave found immediately to the north of the shore temple. It consists of a cave temple, cut into a rock located right on the shore, with the sea waves dashing constantly against it. The northern face of the rock depicts a large, monstrous, club-wielding Mahishasura running for his life. His escape is halted midway by a powerful, menacing lion who pounces from behind on his head and mauls him down. It is a terrifyingly awe-inspiring portrayal of two beasts in instinctive combat. The sculpture, though unfinished, is a masterly artistic visualization of animal combat, the like of which is not to be seen elsewhere. It is evident that Mamallapuram artists were masters in portraying the instinctive qualities of different creatures such as the cow, bull, monkey, elephant, deer, cat, and even rat.

Pancha Pandava Cave Temple

On the southern side, adjacent to the great bas-relief of Arjuna's penance, is the biggest cave temple excavated at Mamallapuram. It is designed as a single-celled temple with a pillared-passage made by tunnelling the rear part of the sanctum. Consequently, the cave has been cut too deep inside, to a depth of about thirty-two feet, while on the north-south lateral axis it measures around thirty-six feet. Probably it was meant to be a square of thirty-six feet. The front part consists of two lateral rows of pillars dividing it into two bays. The

Plate III: Five rathas from the southern end

Plate IV: Dharmaraja ratha known in inscriptions as Atyantakama Pallaveshvara griham

Plate I: Mahishasuramardini panel in the Mahishasura Mardini cave temple

Plate II: Vishnu as Trivikrama in the Varaha cave

sanctum cell is at the beginning of the third bay. Its entrance was about three feet wide. Work on the inner side of the sanctum had probably just begun when it was abandoned. The top of the façade is lined with a row of miniature rectangular square towers resembling temple towers. No inscription or sculpture is found in the cave.

From this cave to the Krishna mandapa, the rocks show attempts to cut some form. The name Pancha Pandava cave temple applied to this cave has no connection with the Pancha Pandava heroes. The story of Mahabharata was so popular that any group of five could be called after the five brothers.

Pulippudar Mandapa

On the western side of the village there are three cave temples in different stages of completion. These have no aesthetic value, but a visit to them can be useful for a better understanding of the Mamallapuram monuments and the ambitions and passions of the creator. Interestingly, each one of these is laid out on a different plan, elevation, and has a different number of shrines. There are no inscriptions on any of them and the work is rudimentary.

Ramanuja Mandapa

Behind the lighthouse, passing through rugged boulders, one comes to another cave temple, now known as the Ramanuja mandapa. This rock cut cave originally had delightful sculptures. The remaining outlines of the chiselled sculptures show the cave was dedicated to Shiva and the central sanctum also contained a Somaskanda sculpture. This cave suffered maximum destruction during the revival of vibrant Vaishnavism in the sixteenth century. The village witnessed new constructions of mandapas like the Krishna mandapa. During that period of revival, the Vaishnava religious marks of *namam*, *shankha*, and chakra were incised on the pillars of some monuments. Probably it was converted into a plain mandapa for the processional deity of Ramanuja, the Vaishnavite seer, which was brought here for audience during festivals. It must be remembered that Mamallapuram was a sacred centre for the Vaishnavas.

Ramanuja mandapa originally had three shrine cells scooped at the rear with a front mandapa-like bay. The three shrines of equal size, were square in form and separated by walls. The central one, projecting slightly into the front mandapa, had a fine image of Somaskanda carved on the back wall. Unfortunately this has been completely chiselled off. All the three cell shrines, too, have been completely chiselled away and the dividing walls have been removed. No trace of sculpture is seen on the two side walls. Traces of paintings in the central shrine indicate that the sculpture was originally painted. It has been surmised that the two side shrines may have contained Brahma and Vishnu, implying that the three shrines were dedicated to the Trinity.

Immediately in front, on the side walls of the cave, are carved the huge shankha and chakra symbols, stylistically attributable to the sixteenth century. There are remains of some structural activity in front of the cave, ostensibly to enlarge and extend the cave by the addition of a mandapa with pillars and beams. Unfortunately, this work too remains incomplete.

An inscription in the Ramanuja mandapa, found between two lion pillars in the front, extolls the greatness of Rudra. The same verse is also found in the Adivaraha cave, Ganesa ratha, and the Dharmaraja mandapa.

It may be necessary at this stage to take note of the religious fervour that gripped the later half of the sixteenth century. It was at this time that the Adivaraha temple was enlarged with the addition of a big mandapa. It also witnessed the addition of a mandapa in front of the Krishna Govardhanadhari bas-relief. The dvarapala and other sculptures were chiselled off in the Dharmaraja mandapa. In all these places Vaishnava emblems were carved on the side entrance walls. Clues to the happenings are perhaps to be found in the inscription of the Vijayanagara period discovered in the Adivaraha temple. The record refers to the festival instituted for Lord Vishnu (Perumal). The temple Sthala-sayana Perumal, in the centre of the village, also witnessed large building activities in the sixteenth century. The gopura and Dolotsava mandapa were also built during this period. The Vijayanagara era witnessed the resurgence of Vaishnavism under the patronage of the raja gurus of the Vijayanagara emperors. It is interesting to note that all the Vaishnava centres in Tamil Nadu received great attention during this period. It was this vibrant Vaishnavism that manifested itself in Mamallapuram in the sixteenth century. Festivals instituted for Krishna and Ramanuja were symbols of this movement.

Tiger Cave

The cave temple at Saluvankuppam, now called Tiger cave (Photo 5), is a flight in fantasy. It is carved out of a thirty-feet high rock facing the sea. A row of mythical lion heads (*vyalas*) are cut in it, arranged in a semi-circle, resembling an aureole (prabha mandala). There is an unfinished attempt to scoop a sanctum in the middle. The temple tries to express something new propelled purely by artistic instinct. A very small-scale model found cut in a rock south of the shore temple seems to suggest that the cave was intended for Goddess Durga. It seems to be an awe-inspiring unique audience hall of Durga, the goddess of victory. Though the art in Mamallapuram is rooted in religious ethos, it is evident that artistic expression and the urge to create aesthetically appealing forms were very important. The emphasis

Photo 5: Tiger cave at Saluvankuppam

on creativity is revealed in all the monuments, nearly forty in number, each one being different from the other in plan, elevation, or mode of depiction. There are nearly two hundred vivid sculptures carved in stone, each varying from the other. It is a fascinating study of the minds and character of the creators of this paradise.

Another sculpture carved in the same rock confirms this stress on creativity. On the northern side of the same rock, a huge seated lion has a square socket carved in the front of its torso. The work is unfinished, but a similar, finished one, exists on a smaller scale in the seashore complex. The majestic lion seated there has an image of the multi-armed Durga seated inside the square socket. This indicates that this was another audience hall of Durga. While the single seated lion here served as a temple abode of the goddess, the multi-headed Yali mandapa in the Tiger cave was another hall. The king visualized his goddess giving audience to him in different halls at different times.

To the right or south of the Tiger cave are two elephants facing the front, carrying circular howdahs on their backs. Inside the howdahs are seated figures, probably portraying the celestial attendants of the goddess. Further south on the same rock is a horse. The portrayal of elephants and horses by the side of the cave temple of the goddess recalls a widespread tradition in Tamil Nadu, of portraying standing elephants and horses of terracotta or stucco.

Trimurti Cave

At the northern end of the main hillock facing west is the excavated cave temple called Trimurti cave. Trimurti means three deities but in general parlance refers to the Hindu trinity of Brahma, Vishnu, and Shiva. This temple, however, has three scooped-out sanctums that contain Subrahmanya, Shiva, and Vishnu. Brahma is substituted by Subrahmanya here. Some scholars identify the first image as Brahma but it represents Subrahmanya. There are two reasons for this theory. Firstly, as is seen from inscriptions and temple distributions in hundreds of illustrations this sculptural form represents Subrahmanya.. Secondly, this sculpture wears a cross-chain across his body. This is clearly a symbol of the warrior god Subrahmanya, the commander of the celestials) and never for Brahma, who is only a Vedic scholar.

The central sanctum has steps culminating in a moon slab, houses a Shiva linga in the centre and a standing image of Shiva on the rear wall. The standing Shiva in the back wall is four-armed, one hand in *abhaya mudra* and one hand resting on the thigh form the main arms, and an axe (*parasu*) and rosary of beads (*aksha-mala*) in the rear arms.

To the right or north of the central sanctum is the shrine of Subrahmanya standing erect in *samabhanga*, with four arms. He is holding aksha-mala and lotus in the rear arms and his front arms are in abhaya mudra and *kati-hasta*. Subrahmanya wears a conical crown adorned by a garland of flowers at its base. This garland, a symbol of victory in battles, is repeatedly praised in early Tamil literature. Besides, the god wears prominent armour called *channavira* across the body, made of Kadamba flowers.

To the left or south of the central sanctum of Shiva is a shrine with the image of Vishnu, standing erect with four arms, carved on the back wall. Vishnu is in his usual attire with abhaya mudra and kati-hasta on the thigh with the main arms, holding the conch and discus with the rear arms.

Besides these three images is a standing image of Durga carved directly on the rock face, south of the three shrines. Durga stands with eight arms wielding shankha, chakra, sword, shield, bell, and abhaya mudra and hand on thigh. She wears a channavira and breast band and stands erect on the head of a buffalo. Above her niche is shown a beautiful *makara torana*. Steps are provided to indicate that it represents an independent shrine for the goddess. While the shrines for the three male gods are decorated with miniature, rectangular, wagon-shaped shikharas, no shikhara motif exists for the goddess. The makara torana itself serves as the tower. It is important to note that Durga is a protector of the gates of temples, forts, and the makara torana is at the entrance. Durga is a powerful goddess bestowing knowledge and victory. Her manifestations are varied. In this portrayal she appears as 'goddess of victory'. Her importance is further stressed by the fact that she appears with eight arms wielding weapons, while all the three male gods in the adjacent shrines are endowed with only four arms. Her sculpture seems to have been originally plastered and painted. Green, yellow, and red colours are still visible on the top corner of the niche and in different parts of her body. Though she has no separate sanctum, all the four deities Subrahmanya, Shiva, Vishnu, and Durga stand in a row almost at the same level. The row of shikharas above the deities indicates that they were considered as shrines. However, a closer look reveals that the main deity of the group is Shiva as his shrine is provided with prominent steps, and the miniature shikharas above are centred around the shikhara of Shiva's shrine. The Pallava temples generally house Shiva lingas in the centre of the sanctum and an image of Somaskanda at the back wall. In this instance, a standing Shiva is noticed on the back wall with a Shiva linga in the centre of the shrine.This cave is interesting as it differs from the other cave temples in form and content, and provides a refreshing insight into Pallava cult-traditions.

A big stone trough is carved in front of the Trimurti cave, probably to store water for purposes of worship.

Varaha Cave

The Varaha cave is situated behind the great bas-relief—Arjuna's penance. One must cross the nearly finished monolith called Ganesa ratha to reach it. The cave faces west and has seated lion pillars to support the roof. It is rectangular (Fig. III) with a sanctum cell scooped out in centre of the rear wall. The sanctum which projects forward is now empty, but the entrance is flanked by dvarapalas on each side. Besides these, there are four panelled sculptures of exquisite workmanship. The north wall has a beautiful group of sculptures with the boar incarnation of Vishnu as the central theme. Facing this panel is Trivikrama panel on the southern wall. The rear walls on either side of the sanctum depict Gajalakshmi on the north and Durga on the south. These four panels are great aesthetic creations that draw the admiration of visitors. As the Varaha is the most impressive of all the sculptures, the cave is called Varaha cave. The central sanctum is empty but the other sculptures associated with Vaishnava manifestations indicate that the cave was obviously dedicated to Vishnu.

The centre of the Varaha panel shows Vishnu occupying the whole space from top to bottom in human form with the head of a

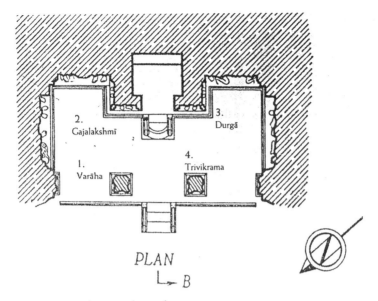

PLAN
L→ B

Fig. III: Varaha mandapa plan

boar (Photo 6). The boar's head is crowned by a tall cylindrical *kirita* made of jewels (*mani makuta*). The Varaha has his left leg planted forcefully on the ground and his lifted right leg is placed on the head of the snake king, Adishesha. Bhudevi, the goddess of the Earth, is seated on the right thigh of Varaha who holds her legs with his left hand. The goddes is seated facing the god with intense love and affection, holding a flower with her left hand and almost fondling the right chest of her Lord. Varaha in turn is fondling her breast with his spout. Two rear arms of Vishnu hold the chakra and shankha, while with the other right hand he embraces the goddess. Adishesha, the serpent king with five hoods, devoutly adores the Lord with folded hands. Beside him stands his wife. The oceanic waters shown as waves and lotus flowers indicate that the scene is enacted in deep waters. Three-headed Brahma stands to the left of Varaha. The right head is damaged. Behind Brahma stands a bearded sage holding a musical instrument, the vina which might represent Narada, the great devotee of Vishnu. Correspondingly, on the right extreme of the panel is a sage with *jata-makuta*, two-armed, standing in *anjali* pose. A stringed musical instrument is placed vertically in front of

Photo 6: Varaha in the Varaha cave

him. Puranic accounts speak of Sage Sunandana singing *sama-gana* when Vishnu manifested himself as Varaha lifting the Earth. Surya and Chandra are shown above on either side.

The image of Vishnu as Trivikrama (Plate II) on the opposite wall shows him with his right leg planted on the ground and the left lifted high above his forehead. He has four hands, three of which hold the chakra, mace, and sword while the fourth is held upwards as if drawing arrows from his quiver. The left hands hold the bow, shield, and conch with the fourth raised and stretched parallel to the lifted foot. Brahma is shown seated on a lotus, in the heavenly sphere, offering worship to the left lifted foot of Trivikrama. In between Brahma and the Lord is seen a bear-headed Jambavan beating a drum; correspondingly, adoring Vishnu is Shiva seated on a lotus. Beneath Brahma and Shiva are seen the Sun and the Moon flying and in the pose of adoring Trivikrama. It is an ingenious way of suggesting that Trivikrama's lifted leg has traversed beyond the spheres of the Sun and Moon and reached the heavenly abode of Brahma and Shiva. On the extreme left of Trivikrama is a crowned figure in human form with a sword in hand falling pathetically from the sky. It represents one of the attendants of the demon king Mahabali who was tossed about by the force of Vishnu's foot when it was lifted up to measure the heavens. The seated figure immediately to the right of Trivikrama is likely to be his mount Garuda. The other figure close to the leg of Trivikrama is Vishnu's devotee Sunandana. On the extreme left is seated a royal figure who is the demon king Mahabali, holding a long-necked vessel from which he pours water signifying a gift. Seated before him, in an extremely agitated posture, is his royal priest Shukracharya.

According to the legend Mahabali was an arrogant demon king who boasted of gifting anything from the world to prove his mastery over the three worlds. To quell his pride Vishnu came in the form of a dwarfish Brahmin boy and begged Mahabali to gift him a piece of land that could be measured in three steps. Mahabali ridiculed this as a small request and agreed. But his guru Shukracharya could see the plot of Vishnu and warned his disciple not to be fooled by the boyish-looking Vishnu who had come to destroy him. Mahabali would not listen and insisted that whatever he had promised he would fulfill, irrespective of the consequences. He offered the boy to take any space he liked that could be measured by his feet. The moment he made the offer the Dwarf assumed a cosmic form encompassing the whole heaven and earth and measured the whole earth with one foot and, with the second, covered the whole heaven and intermediate space. There was no space for the third step. When he demanded place to put his third step, poor Mahabali had no other space and offered his own head. Placing his third step Trivikrama—Vishnu pushed Mahabali to the nether world.

The panel has played another interesting role. The name of the demon king was Mahabali. As this story was well known among the people, and this cave was in the centre of the village, the name Mahamalla was substituted by Mahabali by the common people. The name of the village was hence changed into Mahabalipuram from Mamallapuram from sixteenth century onwards. A local legend was invented saying that this village of Mahabalipuram was founded by the demon king Mahabali Chakravarti. Seventeenth-eighteenth century foreign travellers were told that this village was the creation of Mahabali Chakravarti.

On the side wall by the side of the Varaha panel is carved a lovely image of Gajalakshmi (Photo 7). The two-armed goddess holds a lotus in each hand and is seated on a high lotus seat that emerges from water. Her legs rest in a relaxing pose on the leaf of the lotus. Flanking her are attendant girls. The two girls closer to her carry water in golden pots while those behind them carry garments for the goddess to wear. The scene represents a celestial bathing of the goddess. According to legends, the four-directional elephants including Airavata, the royal elephant of Indra, are said to have bathed the

Photo 7: Gajalakshmi with attendant girls in the Varaha cave

goddess when she emerged from the milky ocean. The elephant to the right of the goddess in this scene could represent Airavata. Durga is seen on the corresponding niche (Photo 8) in the south standing erect with four arms. Her upper hands hold the chakra and shankha, while the lower ones are in abhaya mudra and placed on the thigh. The goddess wears a breast band and a long conical headgear. Above her head is a royal umbrella that symbolizes lordship. Durga is the giver of victory in battles and is the supreme goddess. Her

Photo 8: Durga in the Varaha cave

mounts, a lion and a deer, are shown on the right and left. The goddess combines in her the tenderness of a deer and the robust strength of a lion. A little below are shown two ganas on each side. At the ground level there are two human devotees, one on either side.

It is noteworthy that in Vaishnava temples ritual treatises were followed by the Vaikhanasa texts in Tamil Nadu from very early times. The Vaikhanasa texts prescribe that Shri Lakshmi should be worshipped to the north of the main deity and Harini Durga to the south. The position of Gajalakshmi and Goddess Durga are seen in the same position in two cave temples at Mamallapuram, namely in the Adivaraha cave temple and the Varaha cave temple. This would indicate that the Mamallapuram artists followed ritual treatises in the distribution of icons. This assumes significance when we notice King Rajasimha assuming titles Agama-pramana, one who had Agamas as valid treatises and Agamanusari, a follower of Agamas.

Unfinished Mandapa

Near the Koneri mandapa is another unfinished rock cut cave of almost equal dimensions with two bays. It is not clear as to which deity it is dedicated. The name Unfinished mandapa is misleading as many of the caves are unfinished. There is an attempt to cut a single shrine cell in the back wall, the whole projecting somewhat into the mandapa. The walls were intended for painted stucco images. Four pillars with seated lion motifs can also be noticed in various stages of completion.

The Rathas

There are a total of ten monolith temples cut out of single rocks in different parts of Mamallapuram. The most famous and beautiful monolithic temples are found together in a cluster at the southern end of the village and are popularly known as the 'Pancha Pandava Rathas' or 'The Five Rathas'. Three of the rathas are located at the western end of the village and one is behind the great bas-relief of Arjuna's penance. The last one, in a rudimentary stage of cutting, lies in front of the Mahishasura Mardini cave near the modern lighthouse.

The temples that are the abodes of gods are generally called *Vimana*, that is celestial vehicles. The tradition of shaping the temple structure like a celestial chariot was a popular one. Hence, calling these temples as vimanas or rathas by the people of Mamallapuram is in tune with public perception.

'The Five Rathas' (Plate III) are named after the Pancha Pandavas or the five Pandava brothers—Dharmaraja, Bhima, Arjuna, Nakula, and Sahadeva. They were the heroes of the Mahabharata and have dominated public imagination for a long time. Every village held regular meetings where episodes from the Mahabarata would be enacted or discussed regularly. As such, anything grouped into five used to be named after the Pancha Pandavas. The group of five rathas thus came to be named Pancha Pandava Rathas, even though they are all temples and had nothing to do with the five brothers.

In a way this name is apt for these five monoliths. First of all they are five in number. Among the five rathas, the one on the extreme south is the tallest with three storeys, and presents a dignified look. So it was called Dharmaraja ratha by the people, named after the eldest brother. The second is a rectangular, wagon-roofed ratha, bulky in appearance and appropriately named Bhima ratha. The third ratha from the south is slightly shorter, yet charming, and came to be named after the third brother Arjuna. The fourth ratha at the northern end, resembling a simple thatched hut, houses an image of the Goddess Durga in its sanctum, and hence, is known as Draupadi ratha. These four rathas are in one line running south to north. Another one standing to the west of this group, is an apsidal temple named after the last of the five brothers, as Sahadeva ratha. The five monoliths named Pancha Pandva rathas have a poetic charm rooted in traditional Indian ethos.

Draupadi Ratha

Draupadi ratha is the first temple one encounters upon entering from the village. It is shaped like a thatched hut with a square sloping

Photo 9: Draupadi and Arjuna ratha with a lion in front

roof beautified at the corners with lovely creeper designs. The temple is built on a rock cut platform like the adjacent Arjuna ratha (Photo 9). This platform called *upa-pitham* (sub-base) is supported by figures of lions and elephants.

Inside the *garbha griha* stands Durga on a lotus pedestal with four hands, the upper arms holding the chakra and shankha, and the front arms held in abhaya mudra and placed on the thigh. The goddess wears a breast band. There are two grim-looking pot-bellied ganas on either side of the goddess. At the ground level are seated two heroes, one on either side. The one on the right is in the pose of offering his own head, by cutting it with a long sword, while the other one offers a flower. It seems the goddess is portrayed here as an embodiment of knowledge, in which aspect she would stand erect as a motionless flame in space. Tamil literature assigned to the third-fourth centuries eulogises Durga as the supreme goddess, adored by Brahma, Vishnu, and Shiva. In fact, Durga has been adored as a primordial goddess in Tamil Nadu for a long time.

The Draupadi ratha faces west. A niche containing an image of Durga is carved in each of the outer walls of this temple. On the platform of this temple can be seen a big lotus bud-like carving, which represents the finial, called *stupi*, that is usually placed on top of the tower. Obviously this was made separately and fitted into a socket. A majestic, monolithic, six-feet high lion on a rocky seat adorns the front of this temple. The whole figure is carved in situ. Lion, being the mount of Durga, is normally placed in front of the sanctum of the goddess. It is the artist's clever manipulation to select a standing rock in front of the sanctum to carve this wonderous standing lion.

Arjuna Ratha

Aligned next to and sharing the same platform as the Draupadi ratha is the Arjuna ratha (Photo 10). They even share the same decoration in the Upa-pitham. This west-facing temple is a two-storeyed structure topped by an octagonal shikhara. Such shikharas are known as Dravida shikharas. The temple has a square sanctum preceded by a small projecting mandapa. It is now empty, but the images on the external walls indicate that it was dedicated to Shiva.

The northern wall is decorated with roughly cut sculptures. The central niche houses Shiva with an attendant beside him. At the ground level of the rear wall is a niche showing Subrahmanya seated on an elephant, with a prominent garland of flowers over his head. Indra is also shown here sometimes seated on his elephant Airavata. To the left of Subrahmanya are a bearded priest and his attendant. On his right are two superbly carved apsaras. The one closer to the god is a particularly beautiful depiction of perfect feminine beauty, standing in a delightful threefold bending posture and stimulating a flowing creeper. Her face appears to have an absolutely unparalleled charm, especially when seen in the angular morning sunlight. The brightness on her beautifully delineated face and the sharpness of her eyebrows and eyelids appear fresh even after twelve hundred years. On the southern wall in the central niche stands Shiva in his manifestation as Vrshabhantika-murti, leaning on his mount *Vrshbha*, the bull, Flanking him on either side are two superbly crafted couples.

Photo 10: Arjuna ratha

The well-proportioned figures possess an inviting charm which prompts scholars to think that they may represent gandharvas. The corners show attendants on all sides. C. Minakshi, a Pallava scholar, considers one of the couples as portraying Rajasimha and his queen.

On the walls of the first floor may be seen eight beautiful couples, two in each direction, probably representing the directional deities. The large-sized lotus bud that forms the finial on top of the shikhara is seen placed on the platform as in the Draupadi ratha. Behind this ratha is seen a huge reclining bull (Photo 11). Though incomplete this bull has a charm of its own and is a great attraction for children to play.

Photo 11: The reclining bull behind Arjuna ratha

Bhima Ratha

Adjacent to Arjuna ratha is the huge, oblong monolithic Bhima ratha that derives its name from its size. In this ratha an oblong sanctum was planned with a circumambulatory passage to go around it. The plan was to leave out the corner walls and instead provide pillars supported by squatting lions at the ground floor. The work at that level remains unfinished. But the upper story with sloping roofs and other architectural embellishments are in advanced stages of finish. The side gable ends are very interesting. They show imitation of wood works particularly in the rafter ends. In the centre is a niche topped by a tower-like ornamentation. It looks like a small vimana, square from the base to the neck, tapering into a circular shikhara. The five rathas show five different varieties of vimana towers. This miniature tower, square upto the neck and circular on top is the sixth variety. At the front façade of the Sahadeva ratha is another miniature tower, which is octagonal from the base to the top. Subsequent descriptions of the other monoliths will reveal the differences in each one of them. The ten monoliths depicting twelve different varieties of temple-towers show that there was a deliberate attempt to create variety, which is the hallmark of Mamallapuram.

The Bhima ratha remains an unfinished monument. No worthwhile sculpture or inscription has been found but there are suggestions that this was a west-facing shrine. Its rectangular formation suggests that it might have been intended for the reclining form of Vishnu, popularly known as Anantashayi Vishnu, with some other secondary deities.

Dharmaraja Ratha

The tallest and most majestic monolith stands at the extreme south of the group. It is the three-storeyed monolith called Dharmaraja ratha (Plate IV). It faces west like the other three in its line. From the inscription found here it is known to be a Shiva temple of Atyantakama Pallava (Atyanta-kama Pallaveshvara-griham). This name is found at the entrance to a central cell, on the top floor on the western side, and again on the eastern side entrance lintel of the same floor. Evidently it is the creation of the king who had the title Atyantakama. Various manifestations of Shiva are portrayed on all the three floors. Besides, some forms of other gods are also seen. The three floors represent the three spaces—Earth, Outer Space, and Heaven (*Bhur-Bhuvah-Suvah*). At the ground floor the following manifestations are seen from the north-eastern corner.

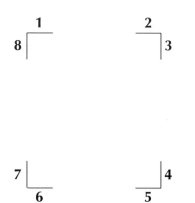

1. Ardhanari
2. Subrahmanya
3. Shiva Trimukha
4. Vishnu
5. Chandrashekhara
6. Bhairava
7. Brahma
8. Harihara

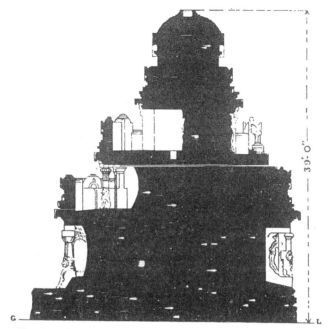

Fig. IV: Dharamaraja ratha section. After Longhurst

The following forms of Shiva are figured in this monolith. These and other forms of dvarapalas, Brahma, Vishnu, Surya, Soma, and Chandikeshvara on the three floors of the monolith would interest students of Hindu iconography.

Kankalamurti, Vinadhara–Ardhanari, Tandava–Shiva teaching dance to Sage Tandu, Chandesanugraha, Gangadhara, Kalari, Harihara, Vrshabhantika, Bhiksatana, Andhakasuravadha, Vinadhara-Dakshinamurti, Nandisanugraha, Somaskanda, Kevala-Chandrashekhara, Vishapaharana, Bhairava, and Kshetrapala.

The Dharmaraja ratha is a three-storeyed square, pyramidal tower, the ground floor being the tallest, the first floor a little shorter and the second floor the shortest of the three (Fig. IV), giving the structure architectural stability. The base of the ground floor is somewhat higher than that of the other rathas in the series. Originally it was planned to provide lateral steps in all the four cardinal directions for the visitors to climb up. The available rock on the northern side is

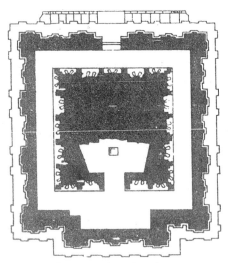

Fig. V: Dharamaraja ratha plan, upper
storey. After Longhurst

cut to provide these steps. Where there was no rock there was a plan
to provide structural steps as seen in the east.

At the ground level, end walls were provided at the corners, with
a central opening supported by seated-lion bases. Two such lions
and two pilasters were provided in each direction. The intention
seems to have been to provide a sanctum on each floor. However,
such sanctums were not fully scooped at the ground and first floors,
though a sanctum had been nearly completed on the second floor.

Each corner wall on the ground floor had a niche housing an
almost life-size standing image of Shiva. Above the sculptures various
titles of King Rajasimha were engraved in Sanskrit in the Pallava
Grantha script. These labels are quite deeply and legibly inscribed but
they are not related to the sculptures below. Iconographically, these
sculptures breathe freshness and mostly do not conform to later
conventional portrayals. All the images found here exhibit tall linear
appearances that qualify as very good examples of Pallava art.

The temple is of a *sarvato-bhadra* variety with square plan (Fig.
V) with openings on all four sides. Once completed the ratha ought
to have had a provision by way of wooden ladders to climb to the
first floor. The ceiling ends of the ground floor are decorated with a

row of miniature square and rectangular towers that garland it and also double up as parapets. The wall of the first floor is recessed, leaving about one and a half to two-feet space to go around in circumambulation. At the western end a half-finished central shrine with a small projecting mandapa can be seen. Of the four sculptures on the western side the pair, immediately flanking the sanctum, are the dvarapalas. The one on the extreme south end houses a lady carrying some offerings in a pot. The one on the north is certainly Shiva's attendant Nandikeshvara with a long sword across his body.

The walls on the side have niches housing images of Shiva. They provide interesting information about iconographical themes and in their distribution some early and rare forms are found. All of them are in standing posture and are about three feet in height. Their aesthetic proportions, the flexions of their bodies, and above all their facial expressions are superb. They are fit to be ranked among the most outstanding creations of the Pallavas. However, due to the narrow space in which they have been created, it seems that an adequate attempt has not been made to illustrate them suitably.

The top floor has a number of sculptures of superb quality. A glimpse of these sculptures can be had from the south side. There is a central shrine, cubical in shape that carries a delightful sculpture of Somaskanda in the centre. Brahma is shown on the right of Shiva and Vishnu on the left, and in the centre of the sanctum is a square socket for installing a linga.

It may be seen that all the central niches in the top floor contain significant sculptures. The west has Somaskanda; in the north is positioned Soma; and the east is the direction of Surya. Judging from this distribution it appears that Shiva's manifestations as Sun, Moon, Agni, and Supreme like Somaskanda occupy their positions on the top floor. The sculpture in the south would therefore represent Kala, that is Death—also identified with Kalagnirudra—or Bhairava. Thus, the whole personality of the temple is revealed by this distribution.

It has been mentioned earlier that this temple has a label inscription which reads Atyanta-kama Pallaveshvara griham. Just as there are inscriptions on the ground floor with titles of Rajasimha inscribed above the sculptures, so also the titles of the king are written above some of sculptures on both the first and the top floors. Almost all

Fig. VI: Dharamaraja ratha, west elevation

these titles are found for Rajasimha Pallava at Kanchi, Panamalai, and other places, indicating that this monolith is a creation of Rajasimha.

The temple has an octagonal shikhara (Fig. VI) and is considered an illustration of Dravida shikhara. The big lotus bud-like carving, the stupi, that tops the shikhara is also found on the ground, on the eastern side of the ratha.

Sahadeva Ratha

It has already been noted that these four rathas are in line. In front of the Arjuna ratha is a lovely monolith in a horse-shoe plan, facing south and almost complete. In Indian architectural treatises such a plan is technically called *gajaprishta*, back of the elephant. As if to suggest this, a standing elephant is carved by its side. Sitting on the back of the elephant it seems that the tower of the Sahadeva ratha also looks like the back of an elephant (Plate V).

These five rathas were mainly intended to portray five different varieties of architecture. With two miniature temple towers appearing as ornamental motifs, one in the gable end of Bhima ratha and the other on the façade of Sahadeva ratha, the author of these monuments managed to create seven different kinds of architecture at this place itself.

Ganesha Ratha

Behind the great relief of Arjuna's penance is situated what is now called the Ganesha ratha (Photo 12). A nearly perfect example of an almost fully-finished monolith, it presents an unbelievably beautiful picture cut in a single rock. Its fine proportions and their articulation show perfection of planning, a superior mastery in cutting monoliths and the unsurpassable skill achieved in converting a rock into delightful imagery. It is a rectangular temple facing west. Since it houses an image of Ganesha in the sanctum it goes by the name Ganesha ratha. The Ganesha sculpture was installed about one hundred and twenty-five years ago. Till then it is said to have had a linga inside with a Nandi facing it outside.

There are no sculptures of merit in this temple but of great significance is a long Sanskrit inscription written in Pallava Grantha script. The record is a repetition of the same verses found in the Dharmaraja ratha and the Atiranachanda cave at Saluvankuppam. The inscription names this temple as Atyanta-kama Pallaveshvara griham after its creator. One of the verses that extolls the greatness of Rudra, found in the Ramanuja mandapa, Adivaraha cave, and Dharmaraja mandapa, is also found here, thus confirming that Rajasimha was its creator.

Photo 12: Ganesha ratha

Valayankuttai and Pidari Rathas

There are three rathas at the western end of the village, one near a pond named Valayankuttai (fisherman's pond), and the other two near the temple of the village goddess called Pidari temple. All the three are unfinished. Work on them had started at the top level and reached upto the ground floor when it had to be abandoned. Two of them face east and the third faces south. Two temples have square shikharas from the neck, but the third has an octagonal one. The square shikharas can be seen only here. There are no sculptures or inscriptions but the work and their shape show the patron's desire to create new forms.

Photo 13: Unfinished monolith in front of Mahishasura Mardini cave

Unfinished Ratha

In front of the Mahishasura Mardini cave may be seen an attempt to cut another monolith. The cutting had started from the top revealing the technique of carving rock cut temples which were started from the top (Photo 13). It also shows another attempt at carving a different monolith.

Bas-reliefs

Arjuna's Penance

Among the most dramatic presentations of scultptural art in Mamallapuram are two bas-reliefs considered exemplary in conception and execution. The first is popularly known as Arjuna's penance (Plate VI) and the other is Krishna Govardhanadhari.

Arjuna's penance (Photo 14) is located behind the central temple in the village and covers a huge rocky surface approximately hundred

Photo 14: Panoramic view of the bas-relief, north wing

feet in length and fifty feet in height. It has an impressive fissure in the centre that seems to play a crucial role in the delineation of the episode depicted. A large number of divine and celestial beings, terrestrial men and animals are portrayed. More than ninety sculptures can be seen on the whole panel. All these figures are shown moving to the centre, towards the fissure, from the sides, presenting a picture of a great river coming down from heavenly heights, passing through the earth and entering the nether world. The rock is vertically divided into two halves. At the top are seen two flying divinities on either side holding their hands in adoration. They are adorned with circular halos behind their heads and represent surya (sun) and chandra (moon). This sphere represents the heavenly region.

Below these scenes, on either side, are shown gandharvas and *vidyadharas* (Photo 15). They are among the eighteen groups of ganas moving through intermediate space. They are known for their beauty and accomplishments in art, music and dance and form the retinue of the gods. They always appear in all monumental art. The panel also shows rishis, *siddhas*, and *charanas* with matted locks of hair and beards (Photo 16). They are associated with slopes of hills and flower gardens.

Photo 15: The sun, the moon, and the celestials in Arjuna's penance

Photo 16: *Siddha*s in Arjuna's penance

There are some long-eared dwarfs and some with their heads covered with cloth. They are known as *Kim-purushas*. Another group, called the *Kinnara* pairs, shown as half-human above the waist and bird below are also part of the troupe. The males are shown with stringed instruments and the females with cymbals in their hands (Photo 17). The Sanskrit tradition ascribes the origin of music to birds. The southern wing of the rock also portrays hunters in the forest and villagers settled on the banks of rivers. The hunters are portrayed as well-built sturdy and bearded men, fierce-looking and holding long bows and arrows, seen moving through trees and forests. They are

Photo 17: Panel showing musicians and lions

surrounded by wild animals like lions, tigers, boars, monkeys, and ant-eaters. The lower part of the panel depicts a Vishnu temple on the banks of the river. There are men at the river, seen bathing, offering daily prayers (Photo 18) or simply sitting in yogic postures. Two lovely male and female elephants are seen moving majestically towards the water. A number of calves are shown playing between the legs of the elephants (Photo 19). The realistic representation of these elephants invariably attracts a lot of visitors. Other animals in the panel include lions, tigers, boars, wild goats, monkeys, rabbits, turtles, rats and cats. In the middle is seen a row of swans flying in formation. From the fissure in the middle emerge *nagaraja*, *naginis*, and snakes to show that they are from the nether world. Further beyond are some ducks.

The central theme of the episode is depicted on the southern wing. Shiva stands majestically, surrounded by his dwarfs, and is seen presenting a weapon (Plate VII). Beside him is an ematiated figure with a long beard. Both his hands are raised and joined above his head as he stands on one leg performing a severe penance. There

Photo 18: A temple of Vishnu with brahmins surrounding in prayer in Arjuna's penance

Photo 19: Elephant calves playing

are differences of opinion about the identification of this scene. Earlier accounts call this Arjuna's penance. But the central cleft fascinated other writers who found in it the descent of the Ganga (*Gangavatarana*). According to the story, the celestial river Ganga came down to the earth with tremendous force, and at the request of Bhagiratha, Shiva agreed to receive the force of the falling Ganga. This episode has been a favourite theme of artists for very long.

According to the legend the ancestors of King Bhagiratha were burnt to ashes and they could attain salvation only on being washed with the waters of the sacred Ganga. Bhagiratha undertook severe penance on the slopes of the Himalayas. Ganga agreed to descend to the earth but, as she would fall with a tremendous force, the earth would not be able to bear her fall. Bhagiratha did penance and requested Shiva to receive the falling Ganga on his *jata*. The waters of the Ganga, after circumambulating the jatas of Shiva, fell to the ground from Shiva's head. This episode, described in detail in the Mahabharata has fascinated great poets and thinkers alike.

Another story narrated in the Mahabharata tells about Arjuna, a hero in the epic. He, at the suggestion of Indra, undertook severe penance on the slopes of the Himalayas in order to obtain the Pashupata weapon from Shiva. Pleased with his devotion, and at the same time to test Arjuna, Shiva appeared as a hunter. Both Arjuna and Shiva killed a wild boar at the same time. A fight ensued between the two. Finally Shiva blessed Arjuna with the weapon.

The descriptions of the slopes of the Himalayas in both these episodes from the Mahabharata are identical, except that in the case of Bhagiratha's penance, the details are greater.

The story of Arjuna receiving the weapon Pashupata has fascinated an early poet Bharavai who wrote beautiful poetry on it named *Kiratarjuniyam*. Bharavai was an elder contemporary of Mahendra Pallava. T.N. Ramachandran, who has examined the scene in detail, suggests that the work of Bharavai directly influenced the Pallava artists of Mamallapuram in the portrayal of this scene and this is not unlikely. Other scholars like Ananda Coomaraswamy have argued for the episode of the descent of the river Ganga.

The fissure in the centre of the Mamallapuram bas-relief is overwhelming in its portrayal of the descent of a river from outer space. However, if the story of Gangavatarana is to be taken as the central theme of the panel then the river should fall on the jatas of Shiva and then descend to the earth. But the panel omits this crucial part of the story. Neither does the river fall on the head of Shiva, nor does it fall from his jatas. Shiva stands on one side of the river, with no connection with the river whatsoever. The theme of the descent of the river is not connected with what is portrayed on the panel. In the case of Arjuna's penance, the central point of the episode is Shiva's presentation of the weapon on the slopes of the Himalayas. This is what is portrayed on the panel, and hence seems to be the most acceptable interpretation of the bas-relief.

Krishna Mandapa

A few yards south of Arjuna's penance is the famous Krishna mandapa, a pillared-pavilion with remarkable sculptures carved on the rock at the back. It is situated behind the living temple in the centre of the village. As it contains the sculpture of Krishna, the Vaishnavas built the mandapa in front in the sixteenth century for celebrating festivals related to Krishna. Originally there was no mandapa, and the carved reliefs were visible as bas-reliefs in the open air like Arjuna's penance. In its original condition it should have been another fascinating group.

The sculptures portrayed here represent a long row of men and women, shepherds and cowherds, and Krishna lifting the hill Govardhana with one hand. All the scultptures are life-sized and carved with exceptional care. Krishna stands majestically as the leader of the group surrounded by *gopis* and cowherds. Some are carrying children on their shoulders, while others lead them by hand. Close to Krishna stands another royal figure, identified as Balarama, the brother of Krishna. Beside him stands a gopi in delightful pose. The cowherds are shown in different postures and one is shown playing his flute and surrounded by a number of cows listening to his music. A cow with its calf standing close by is shown fondling the calf with its tongue affectionately, even as the cowherd is milking it (Photo 1). It is a remarkable scene of tender maternal affection and quite popular among visitors. The cow is venerated in India as the embodiment of motherhood. This scene is immediately contrasted with another one in front of it which shows a majestic bull pompously leading a little calf. Another typical figure is of a milkmaid carrying milk in pots with a rolled mat on her head (Photo 20). By her side is a bearded cowherd carrying a cutting axe with a long handle. In front of the bull is a cowherd couple with their hands clasped in glee. The whole face of the rock portrays a pastoral scene with cows, cowherds and Krishna as their protector.

According to the legend, Indra the king of gods, sent devastating rains and storm to punish the cowherds as they stopped the customary offerings they were rendering him annually at the instance of Krishna. But Krishna came to their succour and lifted the hill, like an umbrella, with one hand and all the cowherds joyfully played and moved beneath it. Indra was brought to his senses. This episode is shown in a very natural manner with the whole hill at the back shown as the Govardhana hill that Krishna lifted.

The side face of the rock shows lions. One of them is shown with a human head and lion's body, recalling the epithet of Narasimha

Photo 20: A milkmaid, Govardhanadhari relief

(man-lion) used by the Pallava king. This portrayal deliberately contrasts with the figures and sculptures of Arjuna's penance where celestials, forest hunters, and villagers are depicted. In the Krishna scene only the clan of cowherds is depicted. This shows a conscious and conscientious selection on the artists' part. Another important point that needs to be noted is that in Arjuna's penance the downward force of the river is taken as the central theme, while in the Krishna Govardhanadhari scene it is the upward force of lifting the mountain that is the central point of attraction.

It would have presented one of the most beautifully figured Govardhana episodes in bas relief had it not been for the mandapa added later in front of it. The artist's painstaking creation gets unfortunately hidden behind the mandapa and visitors are denied the pleasure of seeing it with unfettered vision.

Unfinished Arjuna's Penance

Further south is seen a rocky surface where another attempt has been made to carve Arjuna's penance. This has been abandoned in the rudimentary stage of cutting (Photo 21). Though the outlines of a large number of figures have been carved, the work did not progress, and the whole rock presents a crude stage of artistry. But even from this initial effort it is evident that it would have been another masterpiece.

Photo 21: Unfinished Arjuna's penance

Structural Temples

Seashore Temples

The Seashore temple (Plate VIII and Fig. VII) complex at Mamallapuram has for centuries attracted mariners skirting the shore from Puducheri (Pondicherry) to Chennai and further to the north. The complex consists of three structural temples and a few rock cut sculptures. At present two towers (Fig. VIII) are visible from a distance, the tallest one being a sharp pyramidal tower with a pointed stupi on the east facing the sea. The other is a smaller one facing west, looking like a younger brother of the former. Both these temples dedicated to Shiva were built by Rajasimha Pallava. Sandwiched between them is a Vishnu temple dedicated to the reclining form as Anantashayi. This image and the temple structure covering it were originally carved out of rock. The rest of the structure was built and

Fig. VII: Shore temple, elevation

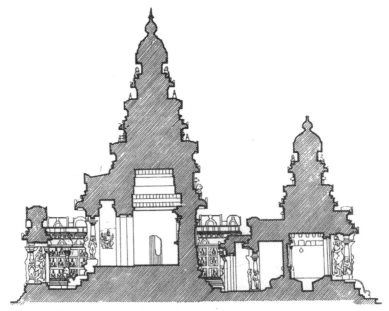

Fig. VIII: Shore temple, section

then dressed with sandstone. While the two Shiva temples were built on a square plan, the Anantashayi temple was constructed on a rectangular plan (Fig. IX). The Vishnu temple also had a rectangular tower, which has since crumbled, with only the portion upto the first tier surviving.

The bigger Shiva temple has a close enclosing wall, which probably had some sculptures. The east facing sanctum of this temple has a tall, highly polished, sixteen-faceted Shiva linga, planted in the centre. At the back wall of the sanctum, a Somaskanda image can be seen. The linga seems to have been displaced and replanted, but with a wrong orientation. The sanctum is preceded by a small ardha-mandapa. The inner wall on the south of the ardha-mandapa has an image of Brahma (facing north) and the northern wall has a sculpture of Vishnu facing south. The outer northern wall of the sanctum is fairly well-preserved and houses sculptures of Tripurantaka Shiva and Durga.

The rock cut image of Vishnu as Anantashayi has four hands. One of the left ones is damaged above the wrist but restored in cement

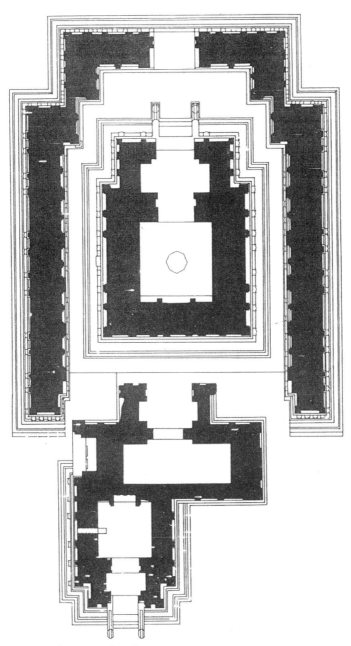

Fig. IX: Shore temple, plan

now. The side walls of this Vishnu temple have sculptures of Krishna *lila*; Krishna felling the demon Kesi in horse form; Krishna dancing on the serpent Kaliya in Kaliya-mardana form (both are in the northern side); and Vishnu on Garuda rescuing Gajendra from the mouth of a crocodile.

The smaller Shiva temple facing west houses a Somaskanda on the rear wall of the sanctum. It also had a linga in the sanctum but that is now missing. This small temple had a small mandapa in the west, which was preceded by a larger one. The bases of these two mandapas have survived but their superstructures are gone. These two mandapas and the temple complex seemed to have had two concentric enclosures. The inner enclosure had a central entrance or *gopura* on the west. There are two sculptures of great significance at this entrance. The one on the south portrays an Ekapadamurti with three heads, one body, and one leg depicting the unity of the Trimurti—Shiva, Vishnu, and Brahma. The other one facing south but found on the northern jamb portrays Nagaraja standing beneath the five hoods of a cobra.

Beyond the entrance on the west there are three fairly large *balipitha*s, or the temple altars, two for the Shiva temples and one for the Anantahsayi temple.

The walls of the enclosure have survived only partially from the bottom but originally had a row of nandis on top of them. All of them have fallen, but the restorers of late nineteenth and early twentieth centuries have rearranged them. The inner walls of the inner enclosure had a series of panels portraying the history of the Pallavas. Some of the surviving panels can still be seen. It is relevant to note that the Vaikuntha Perumal temple at Kanchi, built about fifty years later than the Seashore temple, by the same Pallava king, portrays the history of the Pallavas from its mythical beginnings to the building of that temple. There are label inscriptions that mention the episodes connected with each sculptural depiction. The tradition of portraying the history of a dynasty in a sculptural sequence is first seen in the Seashore temple.

There are a number of inscriptions relating to this temple complex found here. A label inscription found on the lintel of Anantashayi Vishnu Temple, calls it *Narapatisimha Pallava Vishnu griha*.

Narapatisimha is a title of Rajasimha. The balipitha of this temple carries inscriptions in Sanskrit, written in Pallava grantha, extolling the greatness of Rajasimha. All his well known titles are mentioned in them. It is evident that these three temples were built by Rajasimha. Two inscriptions of Rajaraja Chola I dated in his twenty-fifth year, 1010 CE, are found in slabs now inserted into the base of the smaller Shiva temple. They mention the names of all the three temples which are Kshatriyasimha Pallaveshvara-griham, Rajasimha Pallaveshvara-griham, and Pallikondaruliya-devar (Anantashayi). The whole temple complex is called Jalashayana. They also indicate that the rock cut Anantashayi temple was the first to be erected, followed by the other two Shiva temples. The two inscriptions of Rajaraja show that there were flower gardens on both sides of the complex and that all the three temples were under worship even in the beginning of eleventh century CE.

There is much speculation about the Seashore temple. One theory put forward is that there were five more temples with towers that have got submerged under water. Village elders have for very long consistently claimed that they have sighted the metal top of the *kalasha*s. But these speculations have no scientific basis and all that is known is that during some high tides many carved scultpures have been sucked into the sea by the waves. The Archaeological Survey of India formed an underwater exploration wing. Recent studies have revealed that a long rock cut wall, like that of a prakara, is seen jutting into the sea. Probably, some time ago, the sea was a little further away and there was an eastern extension of the prakara. But nothing more has come to light.

An important new discovery was made on the floor of the Shore temple adjacent to the enclosure wall. A small tank-like structure has been uncovered with stone revetments. The centre had a stone-lined well probably used for drawing *abhisheka* water. By the side was found a partly rock cut and partly structural miniature temple, circular in plan and elevation, with a small socket in the centre, housing an image of Shiva as Tripurantaka. The base of this miniature temple is in the form of square, with octagonal and circular plans one over the other, resembling a *yantra*.

The Diving Varaha

The most striking discovery was of a rock cut boar representing Lord Vishnu in his Varaha incarnation. The damaged Boar appears to be pressing its hind legs with great force and bending forward, with its head down as if powerfully charging, ready to plunge into the ocean to lift Mother Earth (Photo 22). According to legend, the Earth was submerged under the deep waters of the ocean and the Varaha dived into the waters and lifted her above the waters. There are many varaha sculptures in India and in most cases the Boar is shown with its head slightly lifted up to suggest that it has lifted the Earth. This is the only illustration where its head is lowered in the act of plunging into the waters. In order to understand this we need to be aware of the situation in which it is located. The artist has placed the varaha right on the coast, on the shore, where the waves dash against it, thus integrating its location and environment, and suggesting that it is

Photo 22: Diving Varaha by the side of the Shore temple

actually diving into the ocean. It is an extraordinary location chosen carefully to make the creation look realistic. This seems to be one of the finest portrayals of not only the varaha, but also of the aesthetic approach of the artists of Mamallapuram.

The selection of monuments such as the Varaha, Arjuna's penance, and Krishna Govardhanadhari reveals that the Mamallapuram artists were great masters at integrating nature and environment into their artistic creations. The varaha is carved on a rocky pedestal bearing the various names of Rajasimha such as Rajasimha, Ranajaya, Shribharah, and Chitra Karmukha in Pallava Grantha characters. The inscription abundantly proves the artistic sensibility of Rajasimha, an 'Ocean of Art' and the patron behind all the creations at Mamallapuram. This sculpture has one more interesting appeal. During the rainy season, or even at high tide, the tank gets filled with water. At that time the boar remains submerged under water, presenting a fascinating spectacle worth seeing.

The Lion Temple

Within the enclosure of the Shore temple, to the south of the triple temple, is a majestic, seated lion, partly carved from a rock and partly sculpted separately and placed in position (Photo 23). In its torso, almost representing its heart, is a square socket serving as a miniature cave–sanctum, in which there is a carved image of Mahishasura Mardini. The lion itself is the temple of the goddess and she is seated in her sanctum. This sculpture suggests the Upanishadic concept that likens the heart to a *guha* (cave) where the Supreme being is said to reside. A beautiful headless deer reclines beside the lion. Between the two stands a headless dwarfish gana.

A few hundred yards away, to the south of the temple, are a few low rocky outcrops. These have also been converted into pieces of art. They are miniature replicas of what has been seen at Tiger cave. They represent a miniature tiger cave, the horse and elephants with howdahs, and a seated lion. These further illustrate the artistic instinct of the patron and his artists.

Photo 23: Seated lion as a temple by the side of the Shore temple

Olakkanneshvara Temple

Right above the Mahishasura Mardini Cave, serving as its crown, is a structural temple built at the same time. Approached by partly built up and partly rocky steps the temple is located at the highest point in the village. Dressed slabs have been used to build this temple, which originally had a tower and shikhara that probably resembled the tower of the Seashore temple. In spite of being in ruins the temple was under worship even in the nineteenth century. The temple now remains from the base to the ceiling with the outer face of the walls exhibiting sculptures. The wall on the south carries a delightful image of Dakshinamurti Shiva. The temple is approached through narrow steps which seem to be the original ones provided during the Pallava reign.

Mukunda Nayanar Temple

On the northern outskirts of Mamallapuram enroute to Saluvankuppam, a small plain structural temple, with an octagonal shikhara, is found half-buried in sand. Known as Mukunda Nayanar temple, it is a Pallava temple of the period of Rajasimha.

Central Temple of Vishnu

In the midst of all these monumental and artistic temples stands the Talashayana Perumal temple dedicated to the reclining form of Vishnu (Anantashayi). This is perhaps the oldest surviving temple in Mamallapuram. Bhutattalvar the fifth-sixth century Vaishnava saint born here, has sung of the greatness of this Vishnu, as has another saint, Thirumangai, who lived in the eighth century. Ever since, this temple has been in continuous occupation as one of the 108 Vaishnavite kshetras. The sixteenth–seventeenth century references to large gatherings of pilgrims at Mamallapuram are mainly due to this sanctity. However, the present structure belongs to the medieval period. The side walls of the entrance of this gopura depict scenes from the Ramayana, and Krishna Lila in addition to Narasimhavatara which transport visitors to the bygone era of the sixteenth century. A tall four-pillared mandapa was built further east on the way to the sea shore for the Dolotsava swing festival. A tank lined with granite steps, with a central mandapa was also built during this period for purposes of sacred bathing and the floating festivals.

The temple is called Talashayana temple in a number of inscriptions found on the walls of the temple. The records refer to the the temple as Sthalashayana and the Lord Vishnu as *Ulaguyya ninra-perumal*, that is 'Lord who stood for the emancipation of the world'. Inscriptions recording grants to the temple are found from the time of the Shambhuvaraya chieftain of the fourteenth century. Late sixteenth century records of Vijayanagara kings are also seen. A point of great historic interest is that the well-known religious saint, Krishnachaitanya Mahaprabhu, paid a visit to Mamallapuram between 1510 and 1512, to worship Lord Vishnu and Shiva in this temple.

Kali

In the midst of the village, behind the shopping street, a raised platform houses the *sapta matrikas*. While most of the matrikas are of the medieval period, the image of Kali is a lovely Pallava (Rajasimha) sculpture. The Goddess is majestically seated. The location of the sculptures with reference to the central Vishnu temple of the village is in the *ishana*, that is north-east. According to the traditional architectural treatises the Vishnu temple should be located in the centre of the village while the temple of the sapta matrikas should be in ishana direction. This confirms that the centre of ancient Mamallapuram was the area of the Vishnu temple. This point still remains the centre of village. It is a fine example of a Pallava village following the textual prescription in its layout.

Lion Seat

Crowning the main rock and serving as the centre of the whole group of monuments is a rock cut, rectangular seat with a reclining lion at one end, serving as a rest. It served as a seat (*Simhasana*) for the patron Pallava king to sit and discuss the progress of the artists. The romantic appeal of the site and the beauty of the surrounding landscape must have fascinated the king as he sat moulding fantasies out of rock.

SIX

Mamallapuram Through the Centuries

An early piece of Tamil literature *Perumban-arruppadai*, extolls a local chieftain called Tondaiman Ilamtiraiyan (first century CE) as the ruler of Tondaimandalam (northern Tamil Nadu), with Kanchipuram as his capital. The text also gives a description of a port under him, and a lighthouse serving as a beacon for seafarers. As Mamallapuram (Fig. X) is praised from the fifth century onwards as a flourishing sea port, it is not unlikely that this is the port mentioned in the early Tamil text.

The Vaishnava saint Bhutattalvar praises his native place as Mamallai, indicating that it was a great port (*ma* meaning great and *mallai* meaning prosperous port). Ever since then, the port has been venerated as a sacred Vishnu kshetra. The Vishnu temple located in the centre of the village predates the Pallavas, though the present structure was rebuilt in the sixteenth century. The village probably received a new name after the title of the Pallava ruler Mamalla Narasimha I in mid-seventh century, when he probably built the Vishnu temple, and called the two Mamallapuram. At the beginning of the eighth century Rajasimha frequently visited this port and commissioned the carvings of the caves, monoliths, open-air sculptures

Arabian Sea

Bay of Bengal

Mahabalipuram
(Mamallapuram)

Shore Temple

Indian Ocean

Fig. X: Map of Mahabalipuram (not to scale)

and structural temples. His inscriptions are found on a number of monuments in this town, proving his patronage.

The awe-inspiring Mamallapuram monuments have for long inspired writers, poets, artists, and tourists. One of them was Dandin, a court poet of Rajasimha, who wrote a purely imaginative novel called *Avanti-Sundari Katha* ('the story of a beautiful girl of Avanti'). He writes of a certain artist called Lalitalaya whose skills surpassed even those of the Greeks who arrived at the court of the king of Kanchi. He invited the king to visit Mamallapuram to see for himself how he had mended the broken forearm of Vishnu from the wrist. The king, probably Rajasimha, and Dandin set out for Mamallapuram. Reaching there they were overwhelmed to see the broken sculpture of reclining Vishnu so carefully and meticulously repaired that even the joints were not visible. This is perhaps the earliest record of scientific sculptural conservation in India. Even as they admired the artistic capabilities of the sculptor Lalitalaya, a miracle occurred in front of them. The sea waves brought a huge lotus flower, which was left on the sacred feet of reclining Vishnu. It immediately turned into a gandharva who rose high in the air. On being questioned about the miracle, the gandharva began narrating the story from which originated the story of *Avanti-sundari-katha*. The story written in Sanskrit was found in a several centuries old manuscript in Kerala.

The next account on Mamallapuram was in the work of another poet but this time the poetry was religious. It was Saint Thirumangai Alvar (mid-eighth)who wrote nearly fifty years after the creation of the monument. He sang in praise of the Vishnu of the Temple of Sthalashayana. Even this religious saint could not escape the appeal of the natural beauty of this shore town and its prosperity due to foreign trade. He praises the prosperous 'Kadal-mallai' which flourished because ships laden with commodities frequented its shores.

An inscription of Nandi Potavarman (Nandi II) dated in his sixty-fifth year (795 CE) is found in the Adivaraha temple. It records a gift of land made by a merchant by the name of Kandan of Mamallapuram.

In the tenth century the Chola emperor Rajaraja visited this town and renamed the township after one of his titles as Jananathapuram alias Mamallapuram. He provided two flower gardens on either side of the Shore temple, with an endowment to supply flowers daily for temple services. His inscriptions are found at the Seashore temple. The two seashore towers are named as *Rajasimha-Pallavesvara-Griham* and *Kshatriya-simha Pallaveshvara-griham*. Rajaraja also provided for the worship of the excavated cave temple at Saluvankuppam. Mamallapuram received great impetus under Rajaraja Chola (985– 1015). A few years after Rajaraja, in the reign of his grandson Rajendra II, an endowment is recorded in the Adivaraha cave, calling the temple *Parameshvara-Mahavaraha-Vishnu griham* (the great Varaha temple of Parameshvara).

In the fifteenth century under the Vijayanagara rulers, Mamallapuram witnessed further prosperity. The main Vishnu temple with its front mandapas and enclosure wall were rebuilt. The Adivaraha cave received a mandapa in front and endowments were made for festivals. The front mandapa of the Krishna Govardhanadhari was added and the Ramanuja mandapa was also repaired. It seems, by the sixteenth century, the Seashore temple had already fallen into ruins but a pathway from the main Vishnu temple to the seashore was laid with some mandapas built at intervals to be used in festive times when the deity was taken to the seashore for the immersion ceremony. The sixteenth century is generally considered as the era, when the Vaishnavite character of the village reached a high point.

An atlas named *Catalan Atlas*, dated 1325 and ascribed to Abraham Cresquas, a Catalonian from Spain, locates a place 'Setemeter' which is identified with Mamallapuram. However, it is not unlikely that the name refers to Sadraspatnam (now called Sadras).

A reference to the Mamallapuram monuments occurs in 1582 in the works of a Venetian traveller who sighted 'eight pleasant hillocks not very high'. His name was Gaspero Babli and he was a jeweller who came to the east for trade. He wrote about this site on his way from Nagappatinam to Santhome. This work has been translated by Purchas into English. He says, 'About three o'clock in the morning we came to a place called "Seven Pagodas" upon which are eight pleasant hillocks, not very high, which are seven leagues from Santhome where we arrived at noon'.

Manucci, who lived in Madras in the seventh century, wrote in his *Storia do Mogor* that 'on the coast of Cholamandal was the sea, and there is also a rock called Mavelivaro, distance four ciagnes from a place called Sadrsta Patao where there are many sculptural fragments resembling Chinese.'

Captain Hamilton, in his *New Account of the East Indies* published in 1727, says that 'near conny-mere are the seven Pagodas, one of which whose name now I forget is celebrated among the Pagans for sanctity and is famous for the yearly pilgrimages made there. The god was very obscene.'

A Frenchman named Sonnerat says, 'The temple called the seven Pagodas which one sees between Sadras and Pondicherry should be one of the oldest on the Coromandal coast, because having been built on the sea coast, the waves come upto the first stage row.'

In 1727, one Charles Boddam, captain of the ship Charlton, brought to India a copper diving engine, together with a diver, in order to investigate the wreck of the Dartmouth cast away at Mahabalipuram six years previously (1721).

William Chambers, who visited Mamallapuram in 1772 and 1776, was the first writer to give a systematic general description of the place and monuments. This was first published in 1788 in *Asiatic Researches*, Vol. I in Calcutta, under the title 'Some Account of the sculptures and ruins of Mavalipuram a place, a few miles north of Sadras, and known to seaman by the name of the Seven Pagodas'. Evidently, the name Seven Pagodas was known among seamen initially. Chambers believed that the Mamallapuram inscriptions were Siamese. In his list of the monuments we find the Ganesha ratha, Arjuna's penance, Krishna mandapa, the structure on the hill of the Mahishasura Mardini mandapa, the Pandava rathas and the Shore temple. Probably the rest were covered with sand then. According to him the 'natives of the place, declared to him that the more aged people remembered to have seen the top of several pagodas, which being covered with copper particularly visible at the sunrise, as their shining surface used then to reflect in sun rays'.

Fra Paolino Da-San Bartholomew who visited Mamallapuram in 1800 wrote: 'But how shall I describe this masterpiece of ancient

Indian Architecture. Never in my life did I behold a work of the like kind. When I visited this place I was attended by five Brahmins who all spoke Portuguese and gave me an explanation of everything I saw'.

In 1798 James Goldenham, an officer under the Madras government, gave more details about Mamallapuram, in *Asiatic Researcher*. He learnt that the great bas relief represented 'Arjuna's Penance'.

Just as the Sanskrit poet Dandin was inspired by Mamallapuram in the eighth century to write fiction, so was an English poet of the western world inspired by Mamallapuram to write an imaginative epic poetry even without visiting this site. A thousand years later it was Robert Southey who wrote his epic 'The curse of Kehama', which is centred around Mamallapuram. Some of the scenes of the epic are located at Mamallapuram.

The first published drawing of Mamallapuram was by M.J. Haffner prepared in 1780, and published in a German book in 1806. His book *Journey to the Coromandal Coast* was translated into French in 1811 and also into English. Subsequently, Haffner wrote that 'whatever one might say about Hindu, one will be convinced on coming to Maweliwarom that this people had possessed in ancient times a great degree of culture and the sciences and that arts have flourished in this country'.

'Idle and Philosophical observer' was the title given to herself by a lady, Martha Graham, who visited Mamallapuram in 1811. Her writings are full of philosophy and poetry about Mamallapuram and are to be found in *Letters on India* published in 1814.

From the seventeenth century a gradual shift is noticed in the character of the village. Some of the appreciative writings on the monumental rock art, sculptures, and temples, started attracting art lovers. When the inscriptions on the walls of the caves were deciphered in the mid-nineteenth century and the Pallavas revealed as the authors of Mamallapuram monuments, the long-forgotten authors of the monuments emerged from obscurity and received greatest admiration from the visitors.

The first serious effort to study the inscriptions of Mamallapuram was made by Benjamin Guy Babington in 1828. He thought it was necessary to connect inscriptions with the monuments for a proper understanding. He read a paper on this in the Royal Asiatic Society in London on 12 July 1828.

James Fergusson was the first to suggest that the Mamallapuram monuments belonged to the period 650–700 in his *History of Indian and Eastern Architecture*, published in 1880, but his revised edition in 1910 gives a still shorter period from 670–700. Mamallapuram entered the Age of Photograhy around 1870. Alexander Hunter, the founder of the Madras School of Arts arranged for photographs of the monuments to be taken in 1871. The photographs taken by him are now in the Madras School of Arts.

The most important work to be published towards the end of the nineteenth century was by E. Hultsch, the government epigraphist for Madras, who published all the inscriptions of Mamallapuram with their English translations in *South Indian Inscription*, Vol. 1, 1892. Hultsch's brilliant analysis of the records helped in clearing many wrong notions about the monuments. Being the first attempt, when epigraphic records were marshalled, there were some errors too in identifying the kings and also in Paleography. For example, about the two inscriptions in the Atiranachanda cave temple, one in Nagari and the other in Pallava grantha, Hultsch held that the two belonged to two different periods, in spite of the fact that both were identical. This view has now been given up.

Similarly, the work of art historian Ananda Coomaraswamy in *History of Indian and Indonesian Art* (1926), needs a revision in the light of subsequent studies. The first half of the twentieth century made steady but slow progress in interpretative efforts, but most scholars were unanimous as far as the dating was concerned. K.R. Srinivasan's *The Cave Temples of the Pallavas*, published by the Archaeological Survey of India, provides a detailed survey of the descriptions of the cave temples at Mamallapuram, furnishing measured drawings of each cave with full illustrations. This remains a major work. Srinivasan followed it up with another work on the Dharmaraja ratha (1975). However, he followed the nineteenth century views of the authorship for the monuments, though he too says that there is no monument of Mahendravarman I at Mamallapuram. Following him, other writers held that successive rulers continued the work on the monuments.

Another work of significance is the article 'New Light on Mamallapuram' by the present author, which analysed the inscriptions and their content and found that all monuments can be ascribed to King Rajasimha. Two renowned scholars on the subject, Stella Kramrisch, an authority on art styles, and D.C. Sircar, formerly Chief Epigraphist for India and an outstanding authority in his field have concurred with the above findings. Stella Kramrisch wrote, 'from the point of view of style, there is nothing to contradict this finding. Also, as a matter of fact, we are at a loss to say stylistic in the work of at Mahabalipuram which also handicap compairing with the sculpture of the Kailasantha temple on account their being overlaid with plaster.' Sircar wrote that 'it seems to be better to regard the Atyanta-kama-Srinidhi-Sribhara-Ranajaya as a single king rather than as two or three different kings as in *Epigraphia Indica*, Vol. X, p. 4 and elsewhere.'

Further studies have appeared from altogether different angles. William Willetts published his valuable work *An Illustrated Annotated Annual Bibliography of Mahabalipuram*. He studied all the writings from 1582–1962, and published the Bibliogaphy which throws abundant light on the Mamallapuram studies. In his conclusion he says that 'this is a published version of the paper read might have been called "Mahabalipuram unwield", since it draws together all the scattered strands of evidence that has been accumulating over the last century, into a stout draw cord with which to pull the shroud from the image of the makers, who stands revealed as Rajasimha. It is the most important contribution to the literature of Mahabalipuram, since the site was first attributed to the Pallavas'.

The great attention has placed Mahabalipuram on the world's tourist map and has since invited thousands of tourists to delight in this marvel of sculptural beauty.

Practical Tips and Information

Mamallapuram has an agreeable climate with temperatures ranging from 20–28° Celsius from January–April. May–August are hot with temperatures reaching from 28–38° Celsius. From the end of October–December is the rainy season.

Mamallapuram is situated near the famous city of Chennai, which is connected to all parts of the world by air, sea, rail, and road. Tourists can stay in Chennai and plan a day-trip to Mamallapuram by road. Two roads connect Mamallpuram to Chennai; the East Coast road, which is short and recently laid according to international standards, and the old Mahabalipuram Road via Thirupporur.

Tourists can also visit the city of Kanchipuram which lies at a distance of about one and a half hours by road from Mamallapuram. Kanchipuram was the most flourishing city in north Tamil Nadu for over two thousand years from the third–seventeenth centuries. It was the capital of the Pallavas and later the northern capital of the Cholas till the thirteenth century, and continued to flourish till the seventeenth century. It is a famous pilgrim centres to this day and according to an ancient saying 'the most beautiful city among all the cities of India'. It has the most beautiful Pallava temple, the Kailashanatha temple built by Rajasimha in 700 CE, and other temples among which Vaikuntha Perumal temple with its Pallava historical sculptures, the great Shiva temple, Ekamranatha temple, and the Vishnu temple of Varadaraja are known for its lovely carved pillared-pavilions. Kanchipuram is also known for it pure silks and its silk-weaving industry. Tourists with limited hours at their disposal usually combine their visit to both Mamallapuram and Kanchipuram on the same day.

Mamallapuram is connected to Puducheri (Pondicherry) by the Southern East Coast Highway and can be reached about one and a half hours.

In 1951 the village was inhabited by only 1,500 people. The population rose to 2,200 in the year 1961, 3,250 in 1971, and to 5,250 in 1981. But within ten years it reached 10,000 in 1991. Its present-day growth is enormous.

Mamallapuram covers an area of 225 hectares of which 70 hectares are used for residential purposes and 85 hectares for trade and petty shops. Out of the 10,00,000 visitors to the town annually, about 5,00,000 are domestic tourists and 60,000 foreign tourists. They usually do not stay overnight here. In addition, another 5,00,000 people from domestic regions visit this town and stay overnight.

Among the residents of this village about 25 per cent are agriculturists, half of them being cultivators and the rest agri-labourers. More than 30 per cent are engaged in petty trades. Modern facilities like roads and street-lighting have improved. Just a century ago people had to come to Mamallapuram by boat through the Buckingham Canal or horse by carts from the nearby town of Chinglepet. It is even reported that one group came by fishing boats from Madras.

The administration of the village is under the control of elected representatives of the town council called the Panchayat. In 1974 it was made into a Village Panchayat and in 1994 it was classified as a Town Panchayat. All the monuments here are under the protection of the Archaeological Survey of India but the control of the surrounding areas is under the Town Council. The government has built a modern shopping complex as close as possible to the five rathas and hopes to move all the petty vendors into the complex. The government has also constituted committees to prepare development plans twice in the past twenty-five years.

All facilities are available at Mamallapuram. There are telephone facilities in the town. The STD code is 04113. There are many tourist attractions around Mamallapuram like: Golden beach and MGM Amusement Park.

One can also visit Dakshina Chitra, an interesting complex that exhibits traditional houses of Tamil Nadu, Kerala, Karnataka, and Andhra Pradesh and their arts and crafts. Traditional craftsmen can be seen practising here. Muttukkadu, a backwater boating yard, crocodile farm can also be visited.

There are numerous comfortable hotels like—Indian Tourism's (ITDC) Ashok Beach Resort, Tamil Nadu Tourism Department's (TTDC) Beach Resort Complex, Heritage Hotel, Fisherman Cove by the Taj Group, Ideal Beach Resort, and Golden Sun.

The site should be seen in the morning. An early visit helps in seeing the monuments rather quietly. From around 10 am in the morning the tourist rush begins that goes upto 6 pm.

The monuments are open to the public from 7 am to 6 pm. A good view of the site can also be obtained from the lighthouse on top of the hill from 2 to 4 pm.

There are special illuminations of the monuments and during the month of January special dance festivals are arranged.

The site is located on the seashore, but the water is rough and swimming is dangerous.

Glossary

abhaya	: gesture of protection
Agamas	: temple ritual texts
aksha-mala	: rosary of beads
alaya	: temple
anjali	: hand gesture held clapped to indicate veneration
ardha-mandapa	: half-hall preceding the sanctum
balipitha	: temple altar
bhuvah	: Intermediate space, sky
brahmanya	: spiritual virtue attained by Vedic sacrifices
chakra	: discus, the weapon of Vishnu
channravira	: prominent armour worn across the body
charana	: one of the 18 groups of celestials
dvarapala	: door guardian
gada	: mace
gajaprishta	: apsidal or horse-shoe plan
garbha griha	: inner sanctum where the supreme deity is enshrined
gopi	: sheperdess
gandharvas	: one of the 18 celestial groups known for beauty and accomplishment in music and dance

gopura	: central entrance
Grantha	: a form of script employed in Tamil Nadu for the past 2000 years to write Sanskrit language
jata	: matted lock of hair
jyotir-linga	: Shiva's symbol of linga representing cosmic flame
kala	: arts
Kaliya-mardana	: Krishna dancing on the hoods of the serpent Kaliya
karanda makuta	: crown resembling reducing size of pots placed one over the other
kati-hasta	: gesture of placing the hand on thigh
Kaumodaki	: name of Vishnu's mace
kim-purushas	: short men with hanging earlobes
kinnara	: a pair of mythical birds that were in human form above the waist and bird below the waist. They always appear as couples, male and female, and are considered best musicians
kirita	: crown
lila	: sport
makara torana	: entrance arch with one crocodile motif on either end
makuta	: crown
mallal	: prosperity
mandala	: circle
mandapa	: pavilion or hall
mishra	: mixed
nagaraja/nagini	: serpent king and serpent queen
Nagari	: script employed generally in northern India to write Sanskrit language
Pallava Grantha	: script employed in the Pallava period to write Sanskrit language from 4th to 9th centuries
Panchajanya	: name of the conch Vishnu holds in his hand
parasu	: axe held in the hand of Shiva
Pashupata astra	: the special and supreme weapon presented by Shiva to Arjuna, the Pandava hero

pitha	: pedestal
prabha	: halo
prakara	: enclosure
prasada	: sanctum tower
rathas	: monolithic temples carved in the shape of chariots
rishis	: sages
samabhanga	: standing erect
shankha	: conch
saptamatrikas	: seven goddesses who are called seven mothers
siddhas	: sages with beard who have achieved mystic powers
shikhara	: tower or peak
Skanda	: Subrahmanya
Somaskanda	: Shiva seated with Parvathi and his child Skanda
stupi	: finial
Subrahmanya	: second son of Shiva
Sudarshana	: name of the discus held by Vishnu
shuddha	: pure
suvah	: heaven
svarna vaikaksha	: golden armour
Trimurti	: the three principal gods of the Hindus, viz Brahma, Vishnu and Shiva
upa-pitham	: sub-base
vidyadhara	: celestial singers who are one among the ratinues of the gods
vimana	: temple sanctum tower
vyala	: Leogrif
Yali	: Leogrif

Further Reading

Banerjee J.N., *The Development of Hindu Iconography*, University of Calcutta, Calcutta, 1956.

Chambers, W., 'Some Account of the Scultpures and Ruins of Mavalipuram', *The Seven Pagodas, Asiatic Researches*, Vol. I, Calcutta, 1788.

Coomaraswamy, A.K., *History of Indian and Indonesian Art*, New York, 1927.

Firgusson, J., *History of Indian and Eastern Architecture*, Vol. 2, London, 1910.

Hultsch, E., 'The Pallava Inscriptions of the Seven Pagodas', *Epigraphia India Vol. X.*, 1909, Calcutta, 1910.

Huntington, Susan L., *The Art of Ancient India: Buddhist, Hindu, Jain*, Tokyo, 1983.

Joveau Dubreuil, G., *Pallava Antiquities*, Vol. 1, London, 1916.

Kramrisch, Stella, *The Art of India*, London, 1954.

_____, *The Hindu Temple*, two volumes, Delhi, 1976.

Krishna, Sastri, 'Two Statues of Pallava Kings, and Five Pallava Inscriptions in a Rock temple at Mahabalipuram', *Memoirs of the Archaeological Survey of India*, No. 26, Calcutta, 1926.

Longhurst, A.H., *Pallava Architecture* in 3 parts, *Memoirs of the Archaeological Survey of India*, Nos 17, 33, and 40, Simla 1924; Calcutta, 1928, 1930.

Minakshi, C., *Administration and Social Life under the Pallavas*, Madras, 1928.

Nagaswamy, R., 'New Light on Mamallapuram', in *Transactions of the Archaeolgical Survey of India*, Madras, 1963.

Ramachandran, T.N., *Kiratarjuniyam or Arjuna's Penance in Indian Art*, Vol. XVIII, Calcutta, 1950–1.

Ramaswamy, N.S., *2000 Years of Mamallapuram*, Vol. I, New Delhi, 1989.

———, *Indian Monuments*, New Delhi, 1979.

Rao T.A., *Gopinatha, Elements of Hindu Iconography*, two volumes, 1915, reprint, New Delhi, 1971.

Srinivasan, K.R., *The Cave Temples of the Pallavas*, New Delhi, 1961.

Srinivasan, K.R., *The Dharmaraja Ratha and its Sculptures*, New Delhi, 1975.

Sivaramamurti, C., *Mahabalipuram, A Guide*, 3rd edition, Delhi, 1972.

Venkata Subbha Ayyer, V., *The Pallavas, South Indian Inscriptions*, Vol. XII, Madras, 1943.

Venkayya, V., *Inscriptions*, XII, Madras 1943. *The Pallavas*, Calcutta, 1909.

Venkoba G., Rao, *Madras Epigraphist Report, Annual Report on S.I. Epigraphy*, for the year ending March, 1923, Madras 1923.

William Y., Willetts, *An Illustrated Annotated Annual Bibliography of Mahabalipuram*, Kuala Lumpur, 1966.

Zimmer, Heinrich, *The Art of Indian Asia*, two volumes, Bollings Series, XXXI, New York, 1955.